CALLSIGN FIVE ZERO

BRIG DEEP BHAGAT, SM

BOLD

An imprint of
Srishti Publishers & Distributors

Srishti Publishers & Distributors
A unit of AJR Publishing LLP
212A, Peacock Lane
Shahpur Jat, New Delhi – 110 049

editorial@srishtipublishers.com

First published by Bold,
an imprint of Srishti Publishers & Distributors in 2026

10 9 8 7 6 5 4 3 2

This is a work of non-fiction based on the author's life and experiences in the Indian Army. While due care has been taken by the author and publisher to verify contents at press time, any inadvertent miss that is brought to their notice shall be duly verified and updated subsequently. Actual names of people and places have been used with a view to provide first-hand information. Names of certain characters, sources and informers have been changed for security reasons.

Printed and bound in India

Contents

Foreword

I first met Deep when he reported to the unit as a young probationer many years ago. Anyone who has served in a Special Forces unit knows that probation is not merely a test of physical endurance; it is a test of character. It is a period when a young officer discovers whether he truly belongs to the demanding brotherhood he has chosen to join.

Deep arrived with a dream of becoming a Special Forces member, like many young officers do. He was enthusiastic, observant, and most importantly, determined to succeed. What made him different from others was his eagerness to learn and his willingness to absorb everything around him. In units such as ours, learning rarely happens through formal lectures. It happens through observation, and often during informal conversations after a long day of training or post an operation.

Young officers watch their seniors carefully. They observe how they conduct themselves, plan operations, lead soldiers, and how they make decisions when circumstances are chaotic. Over time, they begin to understand that leadership cannot be enforced through rank alone. It has to be earned through competence, trust, and personal example.

Deep went on to grow within that environment and eventually led his own troop during a challenging operational period in the Kashmir Valley. The years of counter-terrorist operations in the Valley demanded a great deal of soldierly and leadership qualities. The terrain was difficult, the enemy unpredictable, and the responsibility immense. In such trying circumstances, good leaders found their true calling.

The title of this book, *Callsign Five Zero*, comes from the callsign Deep carried while leading his troop. To those unfamiliar with operational life, a callsign may appear to be a small detail used merely for radio communication. For those who have served in such roles, however, it often becomes associated with moments of intense responsibility and memories that stay with a soldier long after the operation has ended.

In this book, Deep recounts several operational experiences from that period. These accounts are not dramatized or exaggerated in any manner. Instead, they reflect the reality of soldiering. There are moments of tension, uncertainty, and sometimes sheer providence. One such episode, where he narrowly escaped death during an early operation, left a lasting impression on him and eventually became closely associated with the callsign that gives this book its name.

However, the book is not only about operations.

What I found particularly meaningful while reading it were the stories of the men who served alongside him. In Special Forces units, the bond between officers and men is unlike that in most other professions. It is forged through shared hardship and strengthened by trust. Leaders depend completely on their men, and the men expect their leaders to stand with them in every circumstance.

Deep writes about several individuals who shaped his journey – soldiers whose courage, loyalty, and quiet professionalism left a deep impact on him. Some of these stories are deeply moving, reminding us that the strength of a unit ultimately lies in the character of the people who serve in it.

He also reflects on mentors and seniors who influenced his understanding of leadership. In doing so, he touches upon an important truth about military life: none of us grows in isolation. Each officer carries forward lessons learnt from those who guided him and from the men who stood beside him during difficult moments.

What also stands out in these pages is the humility with which Deep looks back on his experiences. Rather than presenting himself as the central figure in every story, he acknowledges many others who contributed to his growth as a soldier and leader.

In recent years, there has been considerable interest among the wider public in understanding the lives of soldiers who serve in demanding operational environments. While popular accounts often focus on dramatic incidents, books like this provide something far more valuable. They offer a personal perspective on the experiences, relationships, and values that shape the life of a soldier.

For young officers who aspire to serve in challenging roles, this book offers an honest glimpse into the mindset required to lead in conditions of uncertainty. For general readers, it provides an opportunity to understand the human side of soldiering – the friendships, the losses, and the lessons that remain long after the operations are over.

Above all, what emerges from this narrative is a deep sense of gratitude towards comrades, mentors, and family members who stand behind every soldier's journey.

Every soldier carries stories from his years in uniform. Only a few choose to record them. Deep has done so with sincerity, and in doing so, he has preserved memories that are both personal and representative of a larger generation of soldiers who served in difficult times.

I am confident that readers will find Callsign Five Zero engaging, thoughtful, and deeply human.

I wish Deep the very best for this book and for the journeys that lie ahead of him

Lt Gen Paramjit Singh Sangha,
PVSM, UYSM, AVSM, SM (Retd)
Former Deputy Chief of Army Staff (Strategy)
9 Para (SF) & 4 Para (SF)

Foreword

The profession of arms is built not merely on doctrine, training, and equipment, but on the courage, resilience, and character of the men who choose to walk its difficult path. The stories that emerge from this profession are often told quietly, if at all, for soldiers rarely speak of their own experiences. Yet, when such stories are recorded with honesty and clarity, they offer invaluable insights into the realities of soldiering and the human dimension of conflict.

I first met Brigadier Deep Bhagat many years ago when I was serving as an instructor at the Infantry School. He had come as a young officer to attend the Young Officers' Course – full of energy, curiosity, and the quiet determination that marks those who take their profession seriously. What struck me even then was his willingness to learn and his eagerness to embrace the challenges of military life.

Earlier, he had been commissioned into my battalion, 13 JAK RIF and it was a matter of pride to see him go on to carve his own path in service of the nation. In time, he chose to volunteer for the elite ranks of the Special Forces, a decision that speaks volumes about his commitment to duty and his appetite for the most demanding assignments.

The ethos of Special Forces is unique even within the already demanding profession of arms. It is built on the principle of voluntary service, where only those who willingly step forward are tested to the limits of their physical endurance, mental resilience, and moral courage. Those who earn the right to wear the insignia do so through relentless training, absolute trust in their comrades, and an unwavering commitment to accomplish the mission, often in circumstances where the margin for error is almost nonexistent.

This book is a reflection of that journey. Through his experiences in counter-terrorist operations in the Kashmir Valley, he provides readers with a rare and authentic glimpse into the challenges faced by soldiers operating in one of the most complex operational environments in the world. These operations demand not only physical courage and tactical skill, but also immense mental fortitude, sound judgment, and a deep sense of responsibility.

The soldiers who operate in the Kashmir Valley do so with remarkable professionalism and restraint, often under conditions of great danger and uncertainty, and their quiet sacrifices seldom find their way into public discourse.

What distinguishes this narrative is its honesty. It does not romanticize conflict, nor does it seek to dramatize events. Instead, it offers a soldier's perspective, grounded in experience, shaped by camaraderie, and guided by an unwavering commitment to the mission and to the men he served alongside.

Books such as this perform an important function. They help bridge the gap between the armed forces and the society they serve. They remind readers that behind every operation are individuals who operate under immense pressure, make difficult decisions, and carry the weight of responsibility in circumstances that few outside the profession fully understand.

I commend Brigadier Deep Bhagat for capturing these experiences and sharing them with candour and humility. His account will not only interest readers who wish to understand the realities of counter-terrorist operations, but will also serve as a source of inspiration for young officers and soldiers who aspire to serve with distinction.

It is my privilege to write this foreword, and I wish this book the wide readership it deserves.

Lt Gen Yogesh Kumar Joshi (Retd)
PVSM, UYSM, AVSM, VrC, SM, ADC
Former Army Commander, Northern Command
13 JAK RIF (PVC**), (Bravest of the Brave)

Author's Note

This book was not written to explain war, justify it, or glorify those who fight it.

It was written to record what stays.

What stays are not dates or operations, but moments—moments when a decision could not be revisited, when certainty was unavailable, and when restraint mattered more than speed. These were not moments of drama, but of attention: noticing a detail, counting rounds, reading silences, trusting another man's judgment without needing to ask why.

Much of what is written here was never taught formally. It was learned later, often under pressure, sometimes at a cost. I have tried to present these experiences without embellishment, because embellishment distorts understanding. Anything that appears exceptional in these pages arose from ordinary people doing their jobs with care, repetition, and humility.

I have been deliberate about including fear and error. Fear is not an anomaly; it is a condition. Error is not failure; it is information that arrives too late. Pretending otherwise serves neither the soldier nor the reader. The men I served with were not fearless—they were attentive. And attentiveness, more than courage, is what keeps people alive.

This book resists neat conclusions. There are no universal lessons here, only patterns that emerge when one pays attention long enough. Some readers may see this as a memoir, others as a manual. It is neither by design. It is simply a record of situations encountered, and responses attempted, written with the benefit of distance but not detachment.

Many lives intersected with mine to make these experiences possible. Commanders who trusted discretion over display. Soldiers who carried responsibility without complaint. Informers and locals who understood terrain, timing, and consequence in ways that outsiders never could. And at home, a presence that made departure possible and return meaningful. Whatever clarity appears in these pages belongs to all of them.

If this book offers anything, it is not inspiration. It is a way of looking at risk, at choice, at one's own limitations. Read it without hurry. Most things that matter do not reveal themselves to speed.

— Brig Deep Bhagat, SM (Retd)

Chapter 1

INTO THE LINE OF FIRE

May, 1996
Dardpora, Kashmir

We had been on our feet for fifteen gruelling hours, trekking through the pitch-dark underbelly of Dardpora's[1] jungle in Lolab Valley. It was raining heavily. We were slipping at every step as we climbed the mountain to approach our target area from the rear. We had taken a detour of thirty kilometres; nobody would expect us to come from here. We had to enter the forest from where no one would watch us. We were entering the stronghold of militants. The Lolab Valley wasn't just a battleground; it was the enemy's so-called 'liberated zone'.

Intelligence reports painted a grim and unsettling picture of Dardpora – a notorious breeding ground for militants. It was a place where insurgents were recruited, trained, and unleashed to carry out hit-and-run attacks on Army posts and deadly ambushes on military convoys. Every path leading to the village buzzed with the constant threat of danger, a hornet's nest waiting to explode.

Our team commander was assigned the mission to penetrate deep into the Dardpora forest, lay ambushes, eliminate the militants, and force them to leave the area. This operation was as much about neutralizing threats as it was a strategy to break the insurgents' grip on the region. This would pave the way for establishing a permanent

---

[1] Dardpora, literally means "abode of pain".

Army post in Dardpora. To succeed, we had to move unseen and strike with precision, knowing full well that the forest could easily swallow us whole if we faltered. There was no scope for error.

Reaching our ambush site was just one phase of the operation, though it was the most critical. For the mission to be successful, we had to ensure that neither militants nor villagers saw or heard us. During the day, villagers roamed freely in the forests with their cattle, making it impossible to move unnoticed. Travelling by night was our only option; the darker the night, the better. The weather was bad, as it was raining, which would fare better for us. We moved under the cover of darkness and concealed ourselves during the day.

I had recently joined the Special Forces unit after completing more than three months of probation. It was a tough experience, and I was relieved that it was finally behind me. I was raring to go, waiting for an operation in the valley. Bravo Team was active in the area, and I joined them as one of the troop leaders. The team comprised three troops, each with around 20 men. I was assigned command of No. 5 Troop, call sign 50 (Five Zero). The other two troops were No. 4 Troop, led by Capt Nirmal Dhaliwal, call sign 40 (Four Zero), and No. 6 Troop, led by Capt Rajeev Krishnan, call sign 60 (Six Zero).

Our plan was straightforward. No. 4 and 5 Troops were assigned to lay ambushes along the forest tracks that the militants were likely to use enroute to the village of Dardpora. These ambush sites were strategically selected on the village's outskirts to intercept any movement. Six Zero, along with the team leader, Major RS Gill, call sign 45 (Four Five), was positioned at a dominating location, providing overwatch and securing the rear. This setup ensured that every angle was covered, thereby minimizing the militants' chances of escape while offering critical support if the situation escalated.

Into the Ambush: A Careful Setup

We had been walking all night, exhaustion creeping in with every step. By first light, we reached the fringes of the village, the sky slowly brightening as a cold breeze brushed against our faces. The rains had stopped. We were drenched in rain and sweat. We needed a place to hide, somewhere that was close enough to ambush our targets. After a tense search, we found a spot which was concealed along the forest track, a narrow path we knew the militants favoured on their way to the village.

The bushes along the militants' route worked in our favour, by giving us excellent concealment. More importantly, time was still on our side.

In the Valley, militants rarely moved at dawn. Early morning was the most dangerous time for them. Army units preferred to operate under the cover of darkness—moving silently through the night and laying ambushes close to villages just before first light. Any militant movement at that hour risked walking straight into a trap.

For this reason, militants never relied on instinct alone. Before stepping out of hiding, they had to be absolutely certain that no Army unit, overt or covert, was lurking nearby. Until then, they stayed put.

This was where the villagers became critical stakeholders in the militants' war. Long before a weapon was raised, they formed the first line of defence.

As they went about their daily routines each morning, they unknowingly, or deliberately, functioned as human detection systems: eyes scanning forest tracks, ears tuned for the unfamiliar, alert to fresh boot prints, disturbed foliage, or anything that hinted at an Army presence. Anything unusual was quietly reported, and the message was spread through hushed whispers and discreet signals. Only after this civilian screen reported an 'all clear' did the militants step out of hiding and move.

This was the unseen battlefield of counter-insurgency where information mattered more than firepower, and where the line between civilian life and combat was thin, shifting, and painfully difficult to define.

This made the villagers our first and most dangerous threat. The key to any successful operation wasn't just intercepting the militants, but deceiving the locals. If they detected even a slightest hint of our presence, they would alert the militants before we could get close. Therefore, our entire strategy revolved around staying invisible to the villagers. If we failed at that, any hope of contact with the militants would vanish before it even began.

The sky was still tinged with the faint light of dawn, promising bright sunshine after an entire night of rain. We knew better than to expect any militant movement before 8 a.m. That gave us enough time to slip into our ambush location, unseen and settled, ready to wait for our targets.

Fortunately, we had stayed clear of the village altogether. There would be nothing to betray our presence. In this game of shadows, invisibility wasn't just a strategy – it was survival.

Half an hour passed after we had settled down. It was quiet until the sound of voices broke through the silence. Two men were approaching from the left side of our front squad, talking loudly, their tones casual, unaware of the invisible eyes that were locked onto them. They could be the villagers. Their path led them straight onto the track in front of the squad. It was the rifles slung over their shoulders that confirmed that they were militants. Oblivious to the danger, they kept walking. In the next few seconds, everything exploded into action.

The Claymore mine was the first to go off. Despite its name, it is less a traditional mine and more a directional weapon. It is designed to fire, not explode randomly. It is a brutally effective weapon. When triggered, it unleashes a powerful blast that hurls hundreds of metal fragments forward in a wide arc, like a giant shotgun fired at once.

The front squad commander detonated the Claymore mine as soon as the militants came in front of the squad. The shrapnel would have hit both militants. The ground seemed to jump beneath us as a cloud of dust erupted, swallowing the entire area. We could feel the concussive force in our chests, and for a moment, everything vanished in a haze. There was just dust, smoke, and silence. The squad was blinded, struggling to see through the fog of debris.

As the dust began to settle, I rushed to the centre of the action.

Commando Mukhtiar Singh was crouched low, his body coiled like a spring, his eyes methodically reading the ground ahead. There was nothing hurried about him—every movement measured, every pause deliberate.

Though barely seven or eight years into service, Mukhtiar carried a maturity far beyond his age. Kashmir had been his classroom, and years of close, unforgiving combat had shaped him into a hardened professional. He was a veteran of countless encounters, forged in the valley's long war, and had fought as the buddy of Maj Sudhir Walia and Capt Arun Singh Jasrotia, a lineage that said more about Mukhtiar than any citation ever could.

In front of him, an AK-47 of one of the ambushed militant's lay abandoned on the dirt, untouched. Mukhtiar hadn't picked it up; his instincts were razor-sharp, always cautious of what might come next.

A hundred metres below us, one wounded militant had stumbled towards the village, screaming at the top of his lungs, "*Maar diya, maar diya!*" His voice echoed through the still morning air, raw with panic and pain. The blast had shattered his senses. His ears were ringing, and shrapnel had ripped into him. The shock had taken hold, but he wasn't down yet.

I crouched beside Mukhtiar, my heart pounding as I asked urgently, "*Kitne the?*" (How many militants were there?)

Mukhtiar's Warnings: The Hidden Dangers

Mukhtiar's head snapped towards me, and in an instant, he raised a finger to his lips, his eyes flashing a warning. The message was clear. Sound could kill us here. I clenched my jaw, realizing my mistake. I had spoken without thinking, my voice cutting through the silence which we desperately needed to maintain. Mukhtiar's experience in battle ran deeper than mine, and I knew it.

In moments like this, silence was survival. After an ambush, any remaining militants—whether wounded or not—could be lying low, waiting for us to slip up. Words, especially loud ones, were dangerous. They could give away our presence, and even our exact intentions. Out here, every sound and every word could cost us our lives.

Mukhtiar picked up the AK-47 lying in front of him and quietly circled back to where I stood. Every step was deliberate, and his eyes and ears were constantly scanning the terrain. As he got closer, he leaned in, his breath barely a whisper against my ear. "There were two guys, sir."

He continued, his voice steady but low. "Both were hit by the Claymore mine. The one in front took the brunt of the blast and is badly injured. He's the one who's running down the hill. You can hear him shouting. The weapon lying here is his. The other one was injured, too, but we lost sight of him with all the dust that kicked up. We don't know where he's hiding."

Even though I heard Mukhtiar, my mind was locked on the militant who fled down the hill. I could hear his agonized screams cutting through the morning air. He wasn't far, and I knew we couldn't let him get away.

If I sprint after him, I can reach him in five minutes. If he is alive and injured, he can be taken as a prisoner, and that would be a wealth of information, I thought. My buddy Sukhdev had come and stood right behind me, waiting for orders. The urgency of catching the militant alive gripped me, and before I could think twice, I lunged forward, straight towards the narrow *nallah* that snaked down the slope.

I had barely taken a step when Mukhtiar moved with lightning speed. He grabbed my wrist in a vice-like grip and yanked me back so hard that I almost lost my footing. I froze, stunned by his reaction. My head whipped around, and I stared at him in disbelief.

What the hell? I thought, confusion and frustration boiling inside me. *How could he stop me like that? Why would he?* My instincts screamed to move, to chase, but Mukhtiar had physically restrained me.

I glared at him; my breath heavy. "What? What happened?" I demanded, my voice low but tense.

Mukhtiar didn't flinch. He leaned in close again, speaking so quietly that only I could hear him. "Sir, the militants took this nallah in front to escape. We still don't know where the second guy is. He could be hiding anywhere along this route. If you go this way, you'll walk straight into his trap."

The weight of his words hit me like a cold wave. He was right. Following that path, I would've been charging straight into my own death.

I gave Mukhtiar a sharp nod. "Got it. Thanks," I whispered. Without wasting another second, I pivoted toward the next nallah, running parallel to the one the militants had used. "Tell the Troop Havildar I'm going down towards the injured militant. I'm taking

Sukhdev with me. I need two more men. Get them down here as fast as you can," I whispered to Mukhtiar.

Mukhtiar gave a crisp nod and turned back towards Havildar Ajit, who was coordinating with another squad positioned on the flank. I took off down the hill, Sukhdev close on my heels, my boots crunching against the uneven ground.

At the same time, Mukhtiar reached Ajit and quickly relayed my instructions. Ajit didn't waste a moment. He turned to Commando Jasbir and Commando Paramjit, who were nearby, their eyes sharp and bodies alert.

"Five Zero has gone down," Ajit told them. "He's new to this environment, full of energy—and that can get him into trouble. Your job is to watch his back. Make sure he doesn't do anything rash. Understood?"

Jasbir and Paramjit exchanged a knowing glance, their expressions hard with determination. "Understood," they replied in unison. Ajit gave a quick nod, his voice low but urgent. "Now move—fast!"

They dropped their rucksacks with the rest of the squad and took off down the hill. Time was against them. They knew I was already two minutes ahead, and they couldn't afford to leave me and Sukhdev exposed for long.

Jasbir sprinted downhill, Paramjit close on his heels, both unaware of the threat waiting ahead. They reached the very spot where Mukhtiar had stopped me earlier—but this time, there was no warning. Mukhtiar wasn't there.

What neither of them knew was that one militant had slipped through the ambush and could now be lying in wait in the nallah below. The ground ahead was primed for a sudden, deadly ambush.

The Militant's Counterattack: A Deadly Burst

It happened in an instant. Jasbir had barely taken five steps into the nallah when an automatic burst exploded from the bushes ahead—

three rounds fired with deadly precision. The surviving militant from the earlier ambush had been waiting, his weapon trained on the slope above, anticipating someone to come down. The rapid crack of the shots shattered the morning stillness.

Jasbir was caught off guard, but only for a split second. Training took over. He snapped his rifle up and fired back instinctively, even as bullets tore into him.

Knowing his position was compromised, the militant wasted no time and disappeared into the undergrowth, retreating deeper into the forest. The exchange lasted only seconds, but the damage was done.

The burst had come from just five metres away. All three rounds had torn into Jasbir's abdomen, ripping through flesh and muscle. The pain must have been excruciating, but Jasbir clenched his jaw, refusing to go down without a fight. He turned back towards the slope, staggering, his hands pressed against his gut, blood seeping between his fingers. Paramjit rushed forward, catching him just in time and dragged him to the mud track above.

Jasbir collapsed on the track, gasping for air, his face contorted in agony. Blood pooled beneath him, his breathing shallow but steady, for now. But he was fast losing strength.

Meanwhile, I was further down the hill, closing in on the injured militant whose agonized shouts had echoed through the forest for the past five minutes. Just as I prepared to make my move, the unmistakable sound of automatic fire rang out above. It was a three-round burst. I froze. We, in Special Forces, never used automatic fire; it was against our training ethos. Instead, we relied on quick, controlled single shots to maintain accuracy and conserve ammunition. The signature staccato burst told me everything I feared: the militant had opened fire.

My stomach churned. I looked at Sukhdev, who was already on high alert beside me. "It's militant's fire, sir," he confirmed grimly. "Something's gone wrong. We need to get back."

There was no hesitation; our priority was clear. Our troop needed us now. The injured militant who had run towards the village and had been shouting all along was not the priority. He could wait. "Let's move!" I ordered, and we took off.

Then came the crackle of Havildar Ajit's voice over the radio, tense and urgent: "Five One for Five Zero. Jasbir's been badly injured. You need to get back immediately. Over." Five One was Havildar Ajit's call sign.

My heart skipped a beat. "Five Zero for Five One. Getting back now. Out." The words left my mouth as I broke into a full sprint uphill, my boots pounding against the earth. Adrenaline surged through my veins, but a creeping sense of dread came with it.

As we ran, sporadic gunfire erupted from the surrounding forest. The militants were regrouping, encircling our position. Our ambush location had been compromised, and now we were the hunted. Bullets zipped past us, striking trees and kicking up dirt. I spotted two militants standing in the open, their rifles aimed directly at us. We were exposed, running targets on the hillside.

I turned to Sukhdev. "Cover me, buddy. I have to reach Jasbir."

Without missing a beat, Sukhdev dropped to one knee behind a tree, his rifle steady. A marksman to the core, this was his element. "Go ahead, sir. I'll make sure they don't get to you. I'll join you soon." His voice was calm and resolute, as if we were back in training.

In the thick of all this action, I had tried not to miss anything that was happening around me. The two militants, emboldened by the advantage of high ground, stood exposed on the hill's edge, firing at us with reckless confidence.

We had already identified both of them as foreign militants. They had spotted us climbing, and I could feel their sights tracking my movement with every step I took. But I also knew that Sukhdev would not waste a shot. His aim was unmatched – solid, precise, and lethal. Even from behind the cover of a pine tree, he could see everything in the sunlight, every glint, every movement. With one of them now focused on me, Sukhdev saw his moment.

Without hesitation, he raised his rifle, steadying it against his shoulder. There was no rush, only practiced calm as he took aim. And then – *tap, tap*! Two shots fired with perfect rhythm, exactly as we'd drilled countless times in combat training.

The bullets hit the militant in the face, and he dropped to the ground. It gave me enough time to reach Jasbir.

I sprinted towards Jasbir, where he lay on the track, every second feeling like an eternity. The sight that greeted me was gut-wrenching. Jasbir was sprawled on the muddy track, gasping for breath, his face pale from blood loss. His hands clutched his abdomen, trying to stem the flow, but it wasn't enough. He was in agony, and yet, there was no fear in his eyes—only determination to hold on.

Mukhtiar had joined us by then, his expression unreadable but his presence steady and reassuring. I glanced at him, my mind racing. At that moment, a realization hit me like a punch to the gut – Mukhtiar had saved my life. If he hadn't physically stopped me earlier, those bullets tearing through Jasbir's belly could have hit mine. His instincts, his experience, had been right all along. He had seen the danger which I hadn't.

The tables had turned so fast. What had begun as a successful ambush by us was now a desperate fight for survival. Both militants had slipped through our trap, and instead of eliminating them, we were now surrounded and under fire. Jasbir was fighting for his life on the ground, and our entire troop was locked in a battle for survival, pinned down by militants who were hidden in the dense forest, even though one militant had been successfully taken down by Sukhbir while providing me cover to get back to Jasbir.

I had trained hard for my initiation into the Special Forces, but this was my first real combat experience. All my learnings of the probation days, on one side, this operation was teaching me some rather hard lessons.

And yet, amid the chaos, I realized something deeper. Every sprint, every fall, every drop of sweat shed during those soul-breaking training days had prepared me for this—*this exact moment*—where I had to stay calm under fire, trust my men, and survive.

And as I knelt beside Jasbir, holding pressure on a wound I couldn't see the end of, one question refused to leave me:

What had shaped me for this moment? And how close had I come to never reaching it at all?

Chapter 2

TO HELL AND BACK

August, 1995
One year before Operation Dardpora

> Before the bullets, there was humiliation.
>
> Before command, there was doubt.
>
> Before Dardpora, there was an ambulance and a decision that almost ended everything.

Our Army didn't prepare us for combat by making us strong; it prepared us by almost breaking us.

My probation began the moment we reached the Unit gate. The physical toughening began from the word go. It was relentless—designed not just to test, but to break us. On the third day, after what felt like an eternity of gruelling exercises, we were summoned by the Probation NCO (Non-Commissioned Officer). The man who was in charge of our training and selection was notorious for pushing us to the edge, and today, he would test us like never before.

"All of you… Get your 20 kg packs ready. You have thirty minutes. You're going for a 20 km speed march," he ordered.

"But, that's not fair, Sahab!" my fellow probationer, Capt Hemonto Panging aka Pango shot back. We had barely scraped through our third day, and now we were being told to march twenty kilometres with twenty kilos of weight on our backs! Pango, just a year younger to me, was known for talking straight.

"Why?" the Probation NCO roared, his voice cold and challenging.

"This is just our third day! We haven't even had time to physically condition ourselves. These marches are meant to come later, after we've built up some strength!" Pango's defiance rang out.

He was right! Speed marches for long distances like 20/30 and 40 kilometres were usually done after at least a month of physical conditioning.

"If it's not logical, so be it! This is probation," the NCO snapped, his eyes narrowing. "If you don't like it, you're free to quit and head back to your parent unit."

The challenge hung in the air, heavy and undeniable. The NCO's job was clear: break us, push us to the brink, and see who backs down.

"Relax, Pango! Let's just do this," I said, trying to sound more confident than I felt.

Physically, I was already on edge. My muscles were tight from the constant strain, and fatigue was gnawing at me like a slow, insistent pull. I could feel the weight of dehydration in my limbs, my throat was as dry as sandpaper. My body screamed for rest, yet I knew the hardest part was yet to come.

The run finally began as the evening shadows stretched across the hilly terrain. By the time we set off, the last traces of daylight had disappeared, and darkness enveloped us. I glanced down at my watch, measuring each kilometre as if I could control the inevitable. The seconds dragged by, mocking my every step. Slowly, I realized the truth: I was moving much slower than I should be. The weight of the pack, the pressure to meet the timings, and the relentless exhaustion weighed on me. I pushed myself harder, but the faster I tried to go, the heavier my legs felt. The need to meet the pass timings was driving me to the edge.

And then, the inevitable happened after 11 kilometres. My body, starved of water and energy, simply refused to comply. My mind had gone blank, my focus was shattered. My knees buckled under the strain, and before I could even react, my chin slammed against the rough, upslope surface of the Jammu-Udhampur highway. The dark night swallowed the sound of my fall as I lay there, stunned, unable to move.

With a shamed mind that was only conscious enough to realize that I was being picked up by someone in the ambulance that was following us, I could see my lifelong dream of becoming a Para Commando shatter before my eyes.

With my rifle slung over my back, I sat there, knees drawn up, my arms crossed tightly, clinging to them as if they could hold me together. My head hung between my arms as I curled inwards, hiding from the world. I couldn't summon the strength to lift my head, not once during that long, jarring journey in the ambulance. My eyes were brimming with tears as my mind tried to comprehend what had just happened.

The crushing weight of doubt settled in my chest like a stone. I kept convincing myself that this was it. "To hell with my dreams!" I was done. "I'll go back to my old life—safe, predictable, and simple. What's wrong with that?" I couldn't silence the whispering voice, "Maybe I'm not cut out for this. Maybe I'm not meant to be a Para Commando, after all. Maybe this is destiny, and I should accept it."

I just wanted to go back to my newly-wedded wife, who would be waiting for me in Lucknow. She belonged to a civil background, and I was sure that she wouldn't understand the difference in various arms and services of the Army. It wouldn't matter to her if I became a Para Commando or stayed in an infantry battalion. I planned to tell her that family life as Para Commando was very tough, and that if I pursued it, we'd never be able to live the simple, peaceful life together that she would have wished for. Lost in myriad thoughts, I was somehow convinced that this would make her say, *"Deep, leave everything and come back. Don't worry, we'll still live happily"*.

Cowardly enough, but in that moment which was tearing me apart bit by bit, I wanted her to be my excuse to quit.

I patiently waited for the clock to strike 11 that night so I could speak with Charu at 1/4th the STD phone call rates, as were prevalent in those years. That would give me ample time to articulate my sentences well so as to force her to take the decision on my behalf. Charu was waiting for my call, as usual.

She heard my scripted ordeal patiently and finally said, "Deep, I have been with you for the last several months. I may not know much about the Army and its Regiments, but I know how much being a Para Commando means to you. I have *shared these dreams in your eyes* that have not let you sleep. I know how much you want to wear the Maroon beret, *and* that is only the privilege of elite forces. So, what you *are saying* today *isn't making* much sense to me. I only know that you are not coming back home without the Maroon beret."

Honestly, it was a bolt out of the blue. These were not just words. It was as if someone was building up steel in my spine and telling me in no uncertain terms that quitting was not an option. I was jolted out of my cowardice. That one conversation changed my entire life. I picked up from where I had almost quit—this time with only one thing on my mind: Excellence.

Two months passed.

The final test was a forty-kilometre speed march. No second chances. No explanations. This was the filter.

Before dawn, we started off with full battle load. Five hours and forty minutes was the benchmark for excellence. Anything slower meant you had survived—not that you belonged.

I didn't negotiate the distance. I didn't argue with the weight. I just ran.

Four hours and thirty minutes later, I hit home base.

It took a moment to sink in. I was more than an hour inside excellent time—a performance that no probationer had achieved before. I didn't celebrate. I didn't speak. I simply stood there, breathing, knowing that quitting was no longer an option.

The Maroon beret was no longer a dream. It was now within reach.

A new, thriving, amazing journey of a Special Forces officer wouldn't have been possible, but for this sweet, simple, shy, civilian lady who stood silently alongside me, taking no credit whatsoever. She gave me a new definition of strong people. This pattern has continued unabatedly thereafter, and today, as I write this chapter of my life, I want to pay a small tribute to her. I would want to dedicate everything that I have achieved in my life to my Powerhouse.

Along with her, I want to acknowledge the umpteen strong women in our lives who stand firm with us, through the crests and troughs, braving the storms and protecting us, silently and without claiming any credit.

Amusingly enough, the first gift Charu gave me after the successful completion of my probation was a black-coloured watch, bought from Calcutta (now Kolkata). She told me, "This will not shine in operations, and it won't make any noise. You can take it on all your missions."

Now, that's thinking like a Commando.

* * *

That run didn't make me fearless; it simply removed doubt.

The journey from the ambulance to excellence was where I learned what it meant to stay when quitting was easier.

A year later, in a forest called Dardpora, I would learn what that certainty was really worth.

Because the mission was far from over, and Jasbir was still fighting for his life.

Chapter 3

A LEADER'S FAITH AND A SOLDIER'S RESOLVE

May, 1996

Certainty doesn't quiet the forest. Nor does it stop the bleeding, or slow the ticking of time when a man is fighting to stay alive. It only steadies your hands when everything else is trying to pull them apart.

Jasbir lay on the track, blood soaking into the mud, while the forest around us came alive. The ambush had collapsed. The militants were regrouping. And what had begun as control was now survival.

This was Dardpora. Not as a test, but as a reckoning.

Chaos on the Radio: A Leader's Composure Amidst Battle

On the morning of 5 May 1996, deep inside the unforgiving forests of Dardpora, the radio came alive.

It wasn't one voice—it was many. Urgent. Overlapping. Unrelenting.

"*Golf One for Five Zero—how is Jasbir? Is he alive? Over.*"

"*One Five for Five Zero—can you get him down to the village? How critical is he? Over.*"

"*Alpha One for Five Zero—we can hear the firing. What's your situation? Over.*"

"*Commander for Five Zero—this is the Brigade Commander. Respond immediately. What assistance do you need? Over.*"

Five Zero was my call sign.

Golf One, One Five, and Alpha One were officers from neighbouring units and Sector Headquarters. The Brigade Commander himself was now on the net. The radio—our lifeline in combat—had turned into a storm of voices, each demanding answers I didn't yet have.

Jasbir was bleeding in the forest.

The militants were still out there.

And every call was pulling me in a different direction.

A burst of automatic fire had torn into Jasbir, the youngest commando in my troop. He had fired back instinctively, buying himself a few seconds, and the militant had disappeared into the undergrowth. Jasbir's abdomen was ripped open, his intestines spilling out. Somehow, through shock and pain that should have dropped any man, he forced them back with shaking hands, pressed his torn belly together, and staggered to the mud track above.

Now he lay there. I had just reached him.

The radio sets—our only link to the rest of the force—were no longer reassuring. They gnawed at my focus. Every crackle felt louder than the gunfire around us, every flicker of the red transmit light a signal flare that announced our position to the forest. Each call that came in wasn't help; it was exposure.

Out here, silence wasn't just comfort, it was protection.

We needed to hear the forest breathe—the scrape of boots on wet leaves, the snap of a twig, the faint shift of a man moving with intent. Instead, the radios kept squawking, drowning out the very sounds that could tell us whether death was already closing in.

The voices on the radio didn't understand where I was. They spoke as if I were seated in a secure command post, free to talk, free to think. But every transmission tore through the jungle like a flare, advertising our position to militants who were already hunting us. What we needed were whispers. What we were getting were echoes.

During operations, we spoke only in call signs. No names. No ranks. I was Five Zero—a troop leader in Bravo Team. Our team leader was Four Five. Those numbers were meant to keep us faceless, focused, and protected. Now, that protection had evaporated.

The ambush had collapsed. The militants had fixed our location and were closing in, their fires snapping through the trees, tightening the circle around us. Jasbir lay beside me in the dirt, his abdomen torn by three bullets. His breathing was shallow, his groans barely audible. Blood pooled beneath him, while each second was measured not in time, but in how much he had left to lose.

There was no ambiguity anymore.

Jasbir had to be evacuated—immediately. His heartbeat was faltering, each second was dragging him closer to the edge, and without IV fluids, I was watching him fade away in real time.

I grabbed the radio and called my team leader. "Five Zero for Four Five, we're in contact. Jasbir is down, he's badly injured. He needs immediate evacuation. Over."

I tried to stay calm, but urgency bled into my voice. My team leader, Four Five, was positioned an hour's march from us, perched on the same hilltop, but at the far end. While we had set ambushes closer to the village, he had secured the most dominating position to protect our rear.

But getting to us was no easy task. Between his position and ours lay dense forests and a militant siege which was tightening by the minute. Breaking through that would require nothing short of a miracle.

Meanwhile, I couldn't wait for help. As I fought to stabilize Jasbir, my mind raced to shore up our defences. Four squads formed a tight defensive circle, eyes trained outwards, every man ready for the next wave.

Claymore mines were set ahead of our positions, poised to turn the forest floor into chaos if the militants pushed too close. Claymore mine was our ace, one of the most effective weapons in a jungle firefight. Once detonated, it would fire thousands of shrapnel, killing anyone within the range. Yet, timing was everything. It had to be fired precisely and at the right moment. It could be used only once.

Our Rocket Launcher (RL), our last line of mobile firepower, had to be deployed with surgical precision. I needed to split the RL ammunition among the squads, thus ensuring simultaneous strikes from different angles, each squad hidden within the towering pines. My mind raced, juggling between distributing the RL ammo and keeping Jasbir alive in front of me. He was slipping fast. I had to get an IV in before his veins collapsed from the blood loss.

I drew a deep breath, forcing my mind to slow down to calculate. The team commander was on his way, but he wouldn't reach us in time. Right now, I was facing a relentless barrage of fire from the militants who had surrounded us. Their fire, though erratic and inaccurate, chipped at the twigs and leaves around us, each bullet like a whisper of death closing in.

I needed silence to think, to plan. But the radio kept squawking, calls pouring in from higher-ups and neighbouring units, oblivious to the hell we were in. I couldn't turn off my radio set, since I had to be in touch with all my squad commanders, as well as my team commander. Each crackle from that cursed radio shattered my focus, each voice on the other end was more of a liability than a lifeline. Every word they spoke threatened to give away our position, and every second I lost answering them, Jasbir's heartbeat grew fainter.

Four Five was seated on top of the hill, preparing to move to my location. His eyes narrowed as he listened to the radio chatter, listening to the same conversation on his radio set. His jaw clenched as he muttered under his breath, "Don't they get it? They shouldn't be bothering Five Zero now."

He knew all too well that in these moments, silence was the difference between survival and disaster. Yet, despite the well-meaning intentions of the voices on the radio, they were doing more harm than good. Some of the calls were from high-ranking officers, one even from the Brigade Commander. Protocol demanded respect; it wasn't easy to tell senior officers to pipe down.

Four Five acted without hesitation. His troop commander's life was on the line, and every unnecessary transmission was a signal to the enemy. He keyed the radio once—not to argue, not to explain—but to impose order.

"This is Four Five for all stations."

The net fell silent.

"Five Zero is in contact. No one is to call him. I repeat, no one is to call Five Zero." There was a deliberate pause. "All stations maintain radio silence until further orders. Break this, and you answer to me."

"Four Five. Out."

The authority in his words cut through the airwaves with absolute clarity, leaving no space for debate or hesitation. The radio chatter ceased abruptly, and was replaced by a profound silence that washed over me like a wave of relief. In that stillness, my racing heart began to settle, and my breath returned to a steady rhythm, grounding me for the task ahead.

Leadership in Action: Empowerment and Trust

The order cut through the chaos like a blade.

The radio went silent. And with that silence came space to think, to listen, to fight. The message was unmistakable: men in contact needed freedom, not interference. Rank didn't matter, only reality did.

Four Five had every reason to panic. His troop was in a running fight deep in the hostile jungle. One man lay critically wounded. Evacuation had to be planned under fire. And I, one of his troop leaders, was new to combat. From a distance, he carried all of it. He didn't flinch.

From where he stood, he imposed order, protected his men, and trusted them to do their job. The calm on the net was leadership, exercised without noise.

He had faith in his men. In me.

Then his voice came back on the radio. It was steady and unhurried.

"Four Five for Five Zero. Continue with your task. Call me when you can. I'm arranging a helicopter for Jasbir. I'll link up with you shortly. All the best. Out."

It lasted barely twenty seconds, and that was all it took.

In the middle of confusion and rising pressure, his certainty cut through. There was no micromanagement. No second-guessing. Just trust—placed exactly where it mattered. He believed I would do what needed to be done, and that belief removed hesitation.

I adjusted my grip on the rifle and looked back into the forest.

The fight wasn't over.

But I was ready.

A Silent Hero: Jasbir's Unseen Battle

At the other end of our team's hierarchy was the youngest Commando, Jasbir, lying on the mud track, gripped by unimaginable pain. His face was ashen, his eyes half-shut, but his spirit shone through. Now was the moment to tend to Jasbir. I slung off my rucksack, placed it beside him, and swiftly rummaged through my medical satchel to pull out an Intravenous (IV) kit. As I prepared to administer it, Jasbir's hand grasped mine, his grip surprisingly firm for someone in his condition. His voice was a low whisper, but his words hit me like a cannon blast.

"*Sahab, mai thik hun. Aap abhi apne defence ko strong karo. Mai aapka intezar karunga. Mujhe kuchh nahi hoga* (Sir, I am alright. Leave me for the time being, go tighten up your defences first. Don't worry, I will wait for you. Nothing will happen to me)."

I could feel my throat tighten with emotion. Raw and pure courage lay before me on that blood-stained mud track. I was new to combat; the adrenaline still surged through me, threatening to tip me into a panic. If Jasbir, in his state, had shown even a hint of fear, I knew I would have faltered. But he didn't. He steadied me, his courage was a lifeline in this chaos. I paused, touched his forehead gently, and whispered, "Thanks, Jasbir. *Tu ruk. Main abhi aaya*. I'll be right back."

Our troop comprised four squads that were arranged in a tight circle, each facing outwards, ready for any surprise attack. The militants could be anywhere, hidden behind the tall pines, waiting for a lapse in our vigilance. I ordered the men to redistribute the limited Rocket Launcher (RL) rounds among the squads to meet any attack with a fierce, simultaneous response. Claymore mines were positioned ahead of each squad's location, thus forming an invisible but deadly barrier.

Most of the men were still unaware of what had unfolded so far. Only Mukhtiar's leading squad had the full picture. I now had to brief all squad commanders on the latest situation and what I expected from each of them.

Fire discipline was critical. Any mistake could cost us dearly. As I crawled from one position to the next, I locked eyes with each squad commander and spoke to them in low, steady tones.

"Listen," I said, my voice firm but calm. "Fire only if you see a target. We can't afford to waste a single round, and we can't risk giving away our positions."

These men were veterans, seasoned warriors who thrived under pressure. They had survived countless firefights. Their fieldcraft was impeccable; they didn't need a lecture from me on when to pull the trigger. But, as a leader, I needed to see it in their eyes – acknowledgment, readiness, absolute control. One by one, they gave me a silent nod, the understanding passing between us without a word.

Satisfied, I moved on, my focus shifting to where Jasbir lay, fighting for every breath.

Jasbir's face contorted in agony, each breath a battle against the searing pain that felt like a thousand knives tearing through him. But he didn't make a sound. Not a single groan escaped his lips, knowing that even the slightest noise could betray our position to the enemy. His lips quivered, and his body trembled uncontrollably, yet his spirit refused to break.

When I finally returned to his side, he looked at me with eyes that held both suffering and unyielding resolve. His voice, ragged and almost pleading, came out in a whisper, "Sahab, please, administer the Morphine. I'm in a lot of pain."

I admired Jasbir. Even in so much pain, he clearly remembered the lessons that the Regimental Medical Officer had taught us – "Make sure you administer Morphine to reduce the pain, only if there's no head injury."

Jasbir was one of the toughest among us, always leading the endurance runs with the relentless spirit of a *Haryanvi* warrior. A veteran of countless battles, he was the kind of soldier who spoke softly but acted with unshakeable determination. I remembered a previous operation when we had a casualty on a hilltop. No one thought we'd be able to get him down alive. But Jasbir did it, carrying the injured soldier on his back, all the way down to the base, step by backbreaking step. From that day on, he had earned my utmost respect.

And now, here he was again, showing the same iron will, fighting for his life with the same quiet courage. Even as the life was draining out of him, he kept his focus on the mission, putting the troop's safety above his own unbearable pain. In his place, I know I would've been trembling, but Jasbir—he kept his chin up, eyes steady, refusing to let a single cry of pain escape his lips.

The Battle to Save a Life

I could only imagine the agony that was coursing through him. Every ounce of my medical training would be put to the test now.

Medical training was a non-negotiable component of the Special Forces selection process, a crucible where we learned to face both minor injuries and life-threatening emergencies. This wasn't just theory; it was hands-on, gritty training. We practiced applying tourniquets to fractured limbs, performed CPR on critically injured patients, administered IV and intramuscular injections, and sutured deep cuts. Our instructor, Regimental Medical Officer (RMO) Capt G.S. Nagi, was relentless in his commitment to our understanding. He didn't just want us to memorize techniques; he ensured that we could execute them flawlessly under pressure. He would make us repeated run drills until we could handle any medical crisis with proficiency and confidence.

Handling gunshot wounds was a crucial part of our training, and Captain Nagi emphasized its gravity. "This is of utmost importance," he would say, his voice steady but serious. "You will encounter gunshot wounds. Remember, administering IV fluids can exponentially increase a patient's chances of survival. In an emergency, your first action should be to start an IV. Ringer Lactate is your best bet for blood loss; its density is similar to that of blood. The goal is to trick the heart into believing it's still pumping blood—it won't know the difference."

Capt Nagi was not only an exceptional doctor, but also an extraordinary soldier, embodying the spirit of resilience we aspired to. His teachings were being put to use today.

I hung the IV bottle from a nearby bush, punctured its top, and tied a tourniquet around Jasbir's left arm. I tapped his arm repeatedly, searching for a vein that seemed determined to stay hidden. Sweat dripped down my forehead as I concentrated and finally found it. The needle pierced his skin, and the Ringer Lactate began to flow, its contents rushing into his body.

The theory may have been just that, but it worked wonders that day. Jasbir's heartbeat seemed to stabilize, and his difficult breathing eased slightly. Along with the IV, I inserted Morphine into his body.

After some moments, Jasbir opened his eyes and spoke, "Sahab, I am feeling better. Thank you so much."

"You will get well, buddy. Four Five is on his way to take you to the village. You will soon reach the hospital too."

Meanwhile, our team leader, Four Five, quickly broke through the dense forest and militant siege, bringing much-needed reinforcements. He organized a stretcher and evacuated Jasbir to the village. The Army helicopter would land in a field nearby to take Jasbir to Srinagar. Jasbir was flown directly to the Military Hospital in Srinagar, his life hanging by a thread. At that moment, every second felt like an eternity. The leader's arrival in time was nothing short of a miracle, thereby allowing Jasbir to cling to the thin thread of life, until he could receive advanced medical care.

By the time the firing died down and the forest finally exhaled, I realized something unsettling.

In Dardpora, Jasbir had nearly lost his life. And without knowing it, I had come just as close to losing mine.

Chapter 4

FIVE ZERO: ON THE BRINK

May, 1996
On the brink of fate

We had survived the morning, but the real storm was closing in. As I reloaded my rifle and looked at my men digging in deeper, I knew one thing for sure, this was far from over.

Meanwhile, Four Five had managed to evacuate Jasbir, whisking him to the nearest helipad for urgent transport to Srinagar. Relief washed over me as I watched them disappear, knowing that Jasbir was finally in safe hands.

My buddy, Sukhdev, who had accompanied me down the nallah, had reached back to his squad location after taking down one militant, while covering my move to reach Jasbir.

I returned to my troop location. We could see the fallen militant sprawled face-down on the track. He was one of the two militants who were firing at us, while I was trying to reach Jasbir when he got shot by Sukhdev. But to our surprise, the second militant hadn't fled as we expected; he was still there, hiding among the dense bushes. Though we held a solid advantage with our firepower, he seemed determined to retrieve his fallen comrade.

With nerves of steel, he would slip out of cover, grab his friend's limp body, and attempt to drag him away. Each time he emerged, our shots rang out, thus forcing him to dive back into the bushes empty-handed. His courage was unmistakable, as he was risking his life over and over again to bring his comrade's body to safety.

Our rounds tore through the trees around him, and I was sure he'd taken some hits, but he persisted.

Then, after several tense minutes of this cat-and-mouse struggle, he stopped coming out. Silence fell over the track. It seemed he had finally realized the futility of his effort or perhaps had been too injured to continue. For the first time in hours, an eerie calm blanketed the battlefield.

An hour later, the forest was ghostly silent. The militants who had surrounded us earlier had withdrawn, and even the second militant we were engaging directly with was nowhere to be seen. We couldn't tell if he had succumbed to his injuries or quietly retreated into the shadows. Through a tangle of bushes, we could still see the lifeless form of his fallen comrade lying on the track, about fifty metres away, an unyielding reminder of the brutal clash that had unfolded in this unforgiving terrain.

As evening approached, the standard protocol required us to retrieve the militant's body and hand it over to the nearest police station. But there was a grim risk lurking beneath the surface. Experienced militants, knowing they might not survive, often booby-trap their bodies to strike back even in death. The method was as cruel as it was cunning: a live grenade, pin pulled and held in place only by their tightly clutched fingers. Or sometimes, they'd remove the pin and position the grenade beneath their bodies, which would be rigged to detonate at the slightest disturbance.

This tactic had claimed lives before. A soldier attempting to lift a body could inadvertently trigger the explosive, with devastating consequences. Aware of the risks, we knew that a thorough check was essential before anyone went too close.

Taking a small team of five men, I led the way towards the fallen militant, each of us fully alert. The body lay just fifty metres ahead, silent and foreboding.

Securing the area was critical before we could get any closer to the fallen militant's body. Lateef and I stayed nearest to the body, while two scouts advanced cautiously, setting up defensive positions to survey everything from the ground ahead to the higher terrain around us. The third guy in the patrol stayed behind, keeping watch over our rear to prevent any threat from sneaking up on us.

With our perimetre secured, we prepared for the next, most dangerous step. We carefully tied a rope around the body, then retreated to a safe distance, taking cover behind a solid tree trunk. Gently pulling on the rope, we tugged the body over, shifting it just enough to test if any deadly surprises were waiting for us. Every inch it moved was a test of nerve, as we disturbed the body from every angle, hoping nothing triggered.

Once we were sure the body was clear, I signalled to the scouts. They returned to transport the body back along the path where we'd laid ambushes that morning, their movements covered by the rear scout who stayed alert for any last-minute threats. Lateef and I held our ground, watching their every step to ensure their safe passage until both men and the militant's body were well out of the kill zone. The job was done, but the tension still hung in the air as we prepared to get back to our rear troop location.

* * *

Lateef and I stood alone in the eerie silence where the body had once been. We needed to get back, but a heavy tension hung in the air like a silent warning. I could feel eyes on us, hidden somewhere in the thick shadows of the forest. As an officer, I knew I was a prized target. My epaulettes[2] marked me unmistakably, and could draw a hidden enemy's focus.

We were the last two men of our patrol, and every instinct warned me against turning our backs. Moving with deliberate care,

[2] The decoration on the shoulders that are indicative of the rank of an armed force personnel.

we began to retreat, never letting our rifles drop from the direction of the threat. We walked backwards, step by measured step, facing the dense jungle that seemed to close in around us. To my left, a steep nallah[3] plunged sharply down; on my right, the hillside rose up, casting deep shadows across the forest floor.

My rifle was trained towards the left, where the threat would most likely emerge. Every motion was by the book. We would stop, crouch low, scan every shadow, and sometimes even fire speculative shots to provoke a response from any hidden assailant. Every backward step felt like moving through a tightening snare, danger lurking invisibly, but all too close.

Then, in the silent press of the forest, something shifted in my peripheral vision, a flicker to my right. I turned my head sharply, and my heart seized in my chest. Just a metre away, half-buried in the thick underbrush, lay a militant. His AK-47 was aimed directly at me, the barrel pointed with deadly intent. In that split second, I was face-to-face with the inevitable.

He lay perfectly still, body pressed into the ground parallel to the track, his rifle resting steadily on his left shoulder. He had waited, disciplined and hidden, allowing my entire patrol to pass without a breath. His camouflage was flawless, merging into the bush so seamlessly that no one had spotted him. Now, with a clear shot, he had chosen his moment, his gaze locked on me, his intended prize.

I experienced a familiar sinking feeling that I generally have while losing a tennis match. The game was out of my hands this time, and I was about to pay with my life. Too bad!

My rifle was pointing in the opposite direction, and it took me an eternity to swing to my right – one thousand nanoseconds. As I turned, I expected the entire magazine of thirty rounds to blow off my head. Not even one bullet would have missed the target.

---

[3] a watercourse, such as a stream, riverbed, or gully.

I was shouting for Lateef while I kept turning. My rifle was fixed on my shoulder. With my heart pounding, I emptied my entire magazine into the militant lying in front of me.

Lateef had taken over from me as I paused and changed my magazine. I was in shock and disbelief to be alive. Why the hell didn't he fire? I kept wondering. The mental trauma of going through such an experience was a nightmare. As I took control of myself, I was thinking of my wife, Charu. She would have been a widow today. What a tragedy it would have been!

I spoke to Lateef loudly, "*Bhai, check kar isse. Fire kyun nahi kiya isne?* Why didn't he fire?"

I was keen on getting answers to this question more than anything else.

Then, we found out how God intervenes.

Divine Intervention

He was the second militant who was involved in the firefight with us. He was surely a brave man and had not fled as we had assumed. He had laid an ambush on the track since he knew well enough that we would be using the same track to check his mate's dead body. A bullet had hit him in his thigh, and he had tightly bandaged it with his turban. Another bullet had struck his rifle, got lodged in its firing mechanism, and made the rifle useless.

Lateef was showing the rifle to me, and I was watching it with utter disbelief. The militant must have pressed the trigger, but the firing mechanism did not allow the bullets to be fired.

During the Dardpora operation, I had come face-to-face with death, not once but twice. The first close call was when Mukhtiar held me back from entering the nallah – a choice that later led Jasbir into its deadly embrace. The second was with the militant whose rifle jammed at the very instant that he fired at me.

* * *

Years later, my family and I were on vacation in Kodaikanal, a serene hill station in South India. We had parked our Tata Sumo near the lake, and while the driver went to get water, I stayed in the passenger seat, gazing at the calm waters.

Suddenly, out of nowhere, a monk appeared. He approached the car, his robes flowing gently in the mountain breeze, and knocked on my window. I assumed he was there to ask for alms, so I lowered the window.

But his gaze was intense, as if he knew something only he could see. "*Beta,*" he spoke, "*Hanuman ji ne jaan bachai hai teri, goliyon se bachaya hai tujhe,*" he said softly. (Lord Hanuman has saved your life. You have been protected from bullets.)

Startled, I looked at him and, as if it were the most natural thing in the world, responded, "*Haan, mujhe malum hai.*" (Yes, I know).

The monk nodded, said nothing more, and turned to walk away, fading back into the crowd as quickly as he had come. He had appeared just to deliver that message, and as I watched him disappear, I couldn't shake the feeling that he had glimpsed a truth far deeper than I had ever shared.

I knew and understood what he said. I knew God had saved my life and that had cemented my faith in the Almighty. I knew there was a guardian angel saving me from harm. I must be His favourite child.

Chapter 5

THE SILENT STRENGTH OF LEADERSHIP

May, 1996
The Success of Operation Dardpora

The operation in Dardpora was a reasonable success. Two militants were killed, and a third one had escaped, though he was severely injured. The militant organization in the area was thrown into chaos, and thanks to our efforts of the previous day, the Army was finally able to establish a post in the village. This move had long been on the General's agenda.

The General Officer Commanding (GOC) of the Division was thrilled, and he invited our battalion's Second-in-Command (2IC), Lieutenant Colonel John de Britto, me, and Maj RS Gill to Division HQ for debriefing. The 2IC had arrived from Udhampur just a day prior.

Division Headquarters was only a short drive from the jungle. The same mountains framed its windows. The same war maps lay open on the tables. The difference was not distance, but visibility. What happened here would never be photographed, never retold with excitement, and never earn applause.

Maj Gill and Lt Col Britto worked exactly the way they commanded—quietly, precisely, without any need to be noticed. They didn't speak about leadership. They practiced it, every day, without witnesses.

This was a first for me to visit Division HQ. A GOC is of the rank of a Major General. I had never met such a senior officer before, and excitement bubbled within me as we stepped into the Divisional briefing room.

The General greeted us with a warm smile and, rising from his chair, addressed the 2IC. "Hi, Britto! How are you? Congratulations on the success of the operation. We have been eager to establish a post in that village, and thanks to your efforts, it has finally happened. Please, tell me how did everything go?" he asked, still talking to Lt Col Britto.

We sat down, and I waited, expecting the 2IC to deliver the briefing. After all, this was his moment to shine in front of one of the most senior officers in the Division.

But to my utter surprise, something unexpected happened. The 2IC spoke to the GOC, "Sir, it's best if Maj Gill briefs you about this operation. He is the team leader and was the one in the thick of things, coordinating the entire operation."

Maj Gill, without missing a beat, calmly nodded and began to brief the General. His demeanour was composed and professional, and his words were precise and focused on the preparations for this mission. He explained how we had moved into Dardpora's dense jungle and the route we had taken to surprise the militants in the area.

As he spoke, I could see the General leaning forward, fully engaged. The room's atmosphere was intense. But then, Maj Gill did something that left me speechless.

He paused and looked directly at the General. "Sir," he said, "the real credit goes to the men on the ground, especially Deep here. He is the one who has been in action throughout the operation. Despite being surrounded by the militants and coming under intense fire from them, he managed to stabilize Jasbir. The two militants killed are also attributed to his troop. Therefore, it would be better if he briefed you about the intricacies of the operation and how everything went about."

I was stunned. In front of the highest-ranking officer I had ever met, Maj Gill shifted the spotlight away from himself and onto me. He didn't need to do that; he was the team leader, and the operation's success was as much his as anyone's. But he did it anyway. It was a moment of silent leadership that didn't seek recognition or praise, but rather elevated those around him.

I thought I was just along for the ride, walking in the shadows of my seniors, soaking in their experience. The idea of speaking directly to the GOC had never crossed my mind.

My heart was racing. Nervousness clung to me as I tried to process what was unfolding. Here were two of the most experienced officers I knew, selflessly pushing me into the limelight when they could have easily taken the credit themselves.

As I began my briefing, I felt a surge of gratitude. As I completed my briefing, the General's eyes turned to me, a smile breaking across his face. "Well done, Deep," he said warmly. "You did an excellent job out there. This is what true leadership is all about: staying calm under fire, making the right decisions when it matters the most. Your actions not only saved a soldier's life, but also ensured the mission's success."

I was too overwhelmed to speak, managing a simple nod in acknowledgment. My respect for Britto and Gill, which was already immense, soared even higher. This episode showed me what it truly means to be a leader. Not just in battle, but in life. It was about selflessness, about putting your team's achievements above your own, and about having the humility to recognize the efforts of those around you.

These men, these officers, they weren't after recognition. They didn't need the spotlight to validate their worth. Their confidence came from a deeper place, one that didn't require acknowledgment from others. It was this quiet strength, this invisible force of character, that made them so different.

That day, I learned that leadership isn't always about being at the forefront. Sometimes, it's about stepping back and letting others shine. And in doing so, you light up a path for your team, by guiding them with a strength that doesn't need to speak loudly to be heard

I left that room feeling fortunate and deeply moved. I had found my place among these men. It was as if destiny had opened a door, and I knew I was on the brink of something much bigger.

The Power of Number Five

Twice in a single day, death had come close enough for me to feel its breath.

The first time, I had almost stepped into the same nallah where Jasbir walked into an ambush, unaware of the militant waiting barely metres away. That path would have led me straight into the burst that had torn him open. It could just as easily have been my evacuation to Srinagar that morning.

The second time came later, quieter, and far closer. A militant had me in his sights. The distance was short. There was no cover, no warning, but then his rifle jammed. That was all.

I had never given much thought to numerology. But that day refused to be ignored. It was 5 May 1996, the fifth day of the fifth month. I commanded Number Five Troop of Bravo Team. My call sign was Five Zero.

None of that explains why I lived. And I don't pretend that it does.

But every year, when the fifth of May comes around, I am reminded of something far more important than luck—how thin is the line between command and casualty, between being a voice on the radio and becoming a name remembered afterwards.

I kept the call sign Five Zero for the rest of my operational career. Not as a charm or a belief, but as a reminder that survival is never owned, only borrowed.

And that day, in Dardpora, I was allowed to keep living.

Reunions and Reflections: A Bond Forged in Battle

Operation Dardpora was far from just an operation. It was an experience that left me with lessons I continue to carry till date.

The men I worked with that day, spread across different levels of the unit, formed an invisible structure on which everything rested. Lieutenant Colonel John de Britto, steady and unflinching. Major RS Gill—Four Five—calm under pressure, precise in judgment. Mukhtiar, instinctive and unassuming. And Jasbir—young, brave, and unwavering when it mattered the most.

They came from different roles, different ranks, different responsibilities. What bound them was not bravado or the need to be seen, but a shared understanding of duty. There was no performance for an audience. No search for recognition. Just men doing what needed to be done, because that was the standard they held themselves to.

Jasbir may never have heard phrases like *ownership mindset* or *taking responsibility*, but he lived them without hesitation. Gravely wounded, he fought to stay alive long enough to protect the rest of us from immediate danger. Mukhtiar, junior to me in rank, did something far harder than following orders; he stopped his officer from making a fatal mistake. He didn't argue. He didn't explain. He just acted.

And Four Five understood something that only real leaders do. He knew when to command and when to step back. By shielding us from noise and pressure, he created space for his men to think, decide, and act. He trusted his juniors not because they were senior enough, but because the moment demanded it.

These actions will never appear in official citations or public narratives. But this is leadership in its purest form, practiced when no one is watching, measured not by applause but by outcomes.

If there is a case study in Operation Dardpora, it is this:

Character reveals itself under pressure, not in comfort.

And leadership is not a title you carry—it is a responsibility you accept, especially when it costs you something.

Jasbir survived, though not without enduring a series of gruelling medical emergencies. His wounds complicated his recovery, but the Army doctors worked tirelessly to bring him back from the brink. Nearly a decade later, I ran into him at a CSD canteen. He was the same Jasbir, his eyes still bright with that indomitable spirit.

"I am so happy to see you, Sahab," he said, embracing me tightly.

"I have never been able to thank you for being my angel that day when I was injured. I have wanted to meet you since I came back to the unit. I was so happy when I heard you were coming back to the unit after your tenure in Commando school." Jasbir had put on some weight due to his injuries, but the heart-warming smile was just the same.

He continued, "Do you know I have displayed your photograph in my drawing room? I tell everyone with pride that this officer is the one who saved my life."

"You are a brave man, Jasbir." I just held him tightly without saying anything more.

I won't deny, but at one point in time, I knew I had almost lost him. And to see that he was alive, speaking, and in good health, was infinitely more than I expected.

Unlikely Reunion in Dardpora

Eight years had passed since that fateful operation. As the 2IC of my new unit, 4 Para Special Forces, I found myself back in familiar territory. I was travelling through Lolab, where one of our teams was stationed, when the thought of Dardpora resurfaced in my mind. I had a few hours to spare, so I decided to visit the Army post at Dardpora, where everything had begun all those years ago. A new Rashtriya Rifles (RR) unit was now deployed there. With permission from Sector Headquarters, I made my way to the post.

When I arrived, the Company Commander stood outside, scanning the surroundings like any seasoned officer. As I stepped out of the vehicle, I introduced myself. "Hi, I'm Lt Col Deep Bhagat. I thought I'd drop by and visit the Dardpora post. This place holds a lot of memories for me. I was here eight years ago, operating in this very area. Back then, we were setting up the first Army post here."

The Company Commander smiled warmly. "It's an honour, sir. I've heard your name before, though we've never met. Weren't you with 9 Para Special Forces?"

"Yes, that's right," I nodded. "I was with the 9 Para Special Forces battalion back then."

He leaned in slightly, his expression curious. "We've got a few surrendered militants with us now. There's one in particular who often speaks of you. He claims that he escaped from you during an operation, though he was badly injured that day."

I felt a jolt of surprise, the weight of the past pressing on me. "Really? Could I meet him?" I asked, my mind racing with thoughts. *Could it be the same operation?* The same militant who had slipped through our ambush eight years ago? Could he be the same man who was shouting '*maar diya, maar diya*' when we had fired our Claymore mine onto the first two militants who had come in front of our squad?

The Company Commander nodded and called for his Company Havildar Major. "Fetch him! Tell him there's someone here who wants to meet him."

I stood there, caught between disbelief and anticipation. My heart raced. I remembered the chaos of that ambush, the blast, and Jasbir's injury. Had this man really survived? The irony of it all struck me. Back then, he had been the enemy, a target to eliminate. And now, years later, we were about to meet under very different circumstances.

Soon, I saw a man step out of the barracks. He was of medium height, with the kind of face that had seen too much of life's harshness. He walked toward me cautiously, but without fear.

"Hi," I called out, taking the first step.

"Hello, sir," he replied, his voice calm as if addressing an old acquaintance.

"Do you know me?" I asked, my curiosity burning.

He gave a slight nod. "Yes, sir."

"How do you know me?" I pressed.

His gaze was steady. "I was the one injured in the operation 9 Para conducted in 1996. I was with another mujahideen when the blast hit us on the track. My rifle had fallen out of my hands, and I ran towards the village. I was so terrified by what happened to me that I later surrendered to the Army."

His words stunned me. *It really was him!* For years, I had assumed he was either dead or lost somewhere in the conflict. And now, here he stood! Alive and calm, no longer the enemy I remembered.

Still in disbelief, I asked, "Tell me everything. What exactly happened that day?"

He recounted the events in detail– the blast, the firefight, and even Jasbir's injury. His story matched ours perfectly, leaving no doubt in my mind.

"What's your name, bhai?" I asked softly.

"Bukhari," he answered.

A strange emotion swelled within me. A mix of relief, gratitude, perhaps even a trace of guilt. "I can't believe this. I could have killed you that day. And yet, here you are! Safe, and now working with the Army."

Without thinking, I stepped forward and hugged him. In that moment, the past melted away. There was no hostility, no resentment;only two men who had been on opposite sides of a war, now standing together as allies.

The irony wasn't lost on me: yesterday's enemy had become today's friend. The line between us had blurred, leaving only the shared reality of survival.

Years later, as I approached premature retirement, my phone rang. It was Four Five.

He had left the Army long before and was now leading Security in the civilian world. There was no small talk. No preamble.

"Would you like to come and work with me?" he asked.

I didn't pause. "It would be an honour, sir," I replied. "I can't think of a better leader to serve under."

Time had passed, uniforms had changed. But the bond had not. Some relationships, forged under fire, don't end when the battle does. They simply find new ground to stand on.

And these moments, these bonds define us long after the smoke clears and the echoes of gunfire fade away.

* * *

To this day, I find myself tracing the lines of the relationships that shaped me. Bonds forged in conflict have a way of staying alive, long after the firing stops.

People often look at my journey and ask where the confidence, the calm, the refusal to quit comes from. The truth is, it didn't begin on that battlefield. It didn't begin with Four Five, or with trust earned under fire. It began much earlier.

Before operations. Before command. Before I understood what leadership demanded in return.

There was another man—one who never sought admiration, never offered comfort, and never softened his standards. His lessons were brutal, his expectations unforgiving, and his influence permanent.

He didn't change my career. He taught me how to think before he taught me how to act.

This is the story of the man we feared, resisted, and eventually understood. The man we called Mad Max.

Chapter 6

MAD MAX

During quiet moments of reflection and reminiscence, as I tried to pinpoint the one guru who truly reshaped my life, my thoughts wandered through a maze of influential figures, each leaving their unique imprint.

Britto, Paramjit Sangha, Arun Jasrotia, Sudhir Walia, Joydeep Sengupta, Bhushan, RS Gill, and Alok Jha are some of the stalwarts who have influenced and changed my life. Yet, all of them came late in my life when I had joined 9 Para.

I found myself yearning to discover the genesis of my transformation. Who was that single individual who transformed me into what I am today? Delving deeper into my past, I found that most of my search engines pointed to one remarkable person from my days at the Indian Military Academy (IMA). He started it all. His memories are as vivid and vibrant as if they had happened yesterday.

January, 1990

It was during my third and final term at the Indian Military Academy, a period I anticipated would glide by smoothly. I thought it'd be just a few months of routine training before graduating quietly and uneventfully. For all cadets transitioning from the National Defence Academy (NDA), the IMA experience was designed to be a mere extension, consisting of only two six-month terms each. After the rigorous six terms at NDA, we believed the tenure at IMA would be a breeze, a simple continuation of what we had already endured. We had faced one challenging term after another at NDA, each one tougher than the last, thus leaving us confident that IMA would offer nothing more than a calm and easy-going environment. Everything seemed predictable and stable, and we convinced ourselves that our time at IMA would remain unchanged.

But then came the hurricane.

The storm had a name: Major Mandeep Singh Sandhu.

Fresh from the battlegrounds of Sri Lanka, nursing wounds both seen and unseen, he was assigned to IMA on a convalescing tenure. His reputation preceded him – a young Captain from 10 Para Commando (Special Forces) promoted to Major, whom we saw jogging slowly and deliberately through the outer circuits of IMA. We watched from a distance, whispering among ourselves, almost feeling pity for the poor cadets who would be assigned under him.

Little did we know that we were those chosen ones. Destiny definitely had plans for us.

In my third term of IMA, I took over as the Junior Under Officer (JUO) of No. 8 Platoon, part of the Zojila Company. We soon learned that No. 8 Platoon would be transferred to the newly-formed Jessore Company, and the Company Commander of Jessore Company would be Maj MS Sandhu. That's when the storm hit, and everything changed.

The academy we had once considered demanding but manageable ceased to exist.

Overnight, it turned into something else entirely. Something less an institution, more a rehearsal for war. Days were punishing enough, filled with relentless routine training, but Maj Sandhu was never interested in what could be endured in daylight. The real instruction began after sunset.

When the rest of the academy shut down, bodies collapsing into sleep, Jessore Company moved out—into forests, nallahs, and open grounds—training in pitch-black darkness. No briefings. No explanations. No allowances. Maj Sandhu never believed he owed us comfort or context. What he gave us instead was far more valuable.

Because the enemy he had fought in Sri Lanka did not operate by parade-ground rules. They moved at night, listened, waited, and killed those who made mistakes.

Silence became our first language. We learned to move without sound, to communicate without words, to trust instinct when sight failed. A snapped twig, a careless breath, the faintest glimmer of light—any one of these could get a man killed. Maj Sandhu treated every lapse as fatal, because in the world he had come from, it was.

The night, he taught us, was both an ally and an executioner. It could hide you or betray you instantly. There was no margin for mediocrity, because mediocrity didn't survive contact with a thinking enemy.

The days offered no relief. The academy routine continued as usual, but every spare minute was consumed by training that was designed to exhaust judgment before muscle. Free time vanished, while recovery was a luxury we were not allowed to depend on. Maj Sandhu wasn't building fitness; he was building decision-making under depletion.

Then came the route marches. Ten kilometres. Fifteen. Twenty. Loads heavier than anyone else in the academy carried. Not to prove toughness, but to make endurance habitual. Because in operations, fatigue doesn't ask permission. It arrives unannounced, and men who haven't learned to function under it make fatal choices.

Slowly, painfully, something changed. These were no longer punishments, they were rehearsals. Every night movement, every overloaded march, every denial of rest carried the same unspoken message: *This pain is cheaper than the one you will pay later.*

Maj Sandhu was not preparing us for the academy. He was preparing us for the day when mistakes would be paid for in blood.

The nickname came first – *Mad Max*. It travelled faster than any official notice, whispered across the academy in corridors, on tracks, and in quiet corners after lights-out. With it came an understanding that something different, and deliberately harder, was unfolding in Jessore Company.

The rest of the academy watched us with a mix of unease and reluctant respect. It wasn't just the physical grind that set us apart. It was the psychological weight, the sense that we were being pushed into territory which the academy itself had not planned to enter.

Whenever cadets from Jessore Company crossed paths with drill instructors, appointment holders, or officers from other companies, the reaction was often the same. A pause, a glance, and then a dismissal.

"Oh… you're from Jessore Company. That's enough for today."

No punishments. No extra drills. Not out of kindness, but out of recognition—an unspoken admission that whatever was happening under Major Sandhu was already punishment enough.

Among fellow cadets, the response was quieter. Heads shook. Wry smiles followed. "If you can, get some sleep," they would say, not joking, not mocking, almost respectfully.

That response said more than any formal acknowledgment ever could. While the rest of the academy followed the syllabus, Jessore Company was being shaped for something beyond it.

Under Major Sandhu, there were no shortcuts, and not because he enjoyed denying comfort, but because he knew comfort would never be available where we were headed. Every drill, every movement, was designed to exhaust excuses before it built endurance.

Camp Chindits was among the toughest exercises in the final term. For most of the academy, surviving it once was considered achievement enough. For Jessore Company, that wasn't even the beginning.

We went through it three times – once before the camp, once during it, and once again after everyone else had moved on. Preparation, execution, review, repeat. Over and over, until the body stopped asking *why* and the mind stopped negotiating *how much is enough*.

This wasn't just training; this was conditioning.

Something changed in the process. The resistance faded first. Then the complaints. Finally, the fear. Our bodies adapted, but more importantly, our judgment sharpened. We began to listen, not out of obedience, but because his methods started to make sense. Major Sandhu didn't instruct; he *imprinted*. Every story he told carried the weight of experience, not theory. His lessons didn't explain comfort; they explained survival.

Then he set his next target. "I want the Cross-Country Trophy."

There was no speech. No motivation. Just a statement of intent.

That trophy was the academy's benchmark for endurance. Winning it meant sacrificing free time, rest days, and recovery. He took away our Sundays first. Then our evenings. Then whatever space we still thought belonged to us.

We ran before PT. We ran after games. We ran when the legs begged for rest and the lungs burned for air. Walking was not an option. Pausing was a failure. Shortcuts did not exist in his vocabulary.

Every mile stripped something away—comfort, complacency, doubt. What remained was discipline. The quiet, stubborn kind of discipline that keeps moving when the body is done.

When Jessore Company won the Cross-Country Trophy, it felt almost inevitable. And when we won it again, and again, the pattern became clear. Seven consecutive terms.

But the real victory wasn't the trophy. It was what the process had done to us. We had learned to endure without drama, to push without bargaining, and to trust the grind.

Winning stopped being the goal.

The standard became the reward.

He gave us a value system that went far beyond any written military code.

"Talk straight," he would say.

"Don't dodge the truth. Choose the harder right over the easier wrong. Own your mistakes. Look after your buddy. Secure yourself first, only then rest."

He didn't repeat these as slogans, but helped us to enforce them as a way of life.

And then came his most unsettling lesson – *think*. Question everything. Even authority. Especially authority.

"Never take anything at face value," he told us. "Not even my orders."

That single instruction separated us from the rest. It made us uncomfortable, difficult, and unwilling to accept mediocrity. We became men who asked *why* when others were content with *because*. Rebels, not against the system, more against the laziness of thought.

And there was a price to be paid. We didn't blend in easily. We were called difficult. Unmanageable. Unfit for 'normal' environments. Many of us would never rise smoothly through polite hierarchies. But what we gained mattered more than rank: an unshakeable sense of self and the courage to stand by it.

Without him, the idea of joining the Special Forces might never have taken root in my mind. I would have continued to see them as men of brute strength and physical excess. He was the one who revealed the truth that beneath the muscle and grit lies something far more dangerous – a thinking mind.

The best warriors, he showed us, are not those who crave war. They are those who understand it deeply enough to prevent it. And when forced into it, dominate it decisively, and then disappear.

To the world, he was Major Mandeep Singh Sandhu. To us, he was Mad Max.

Not because he broke us, but because he refused to let us remain ordinary.

I admired him without reservation, and feared him just as deeply. Not because he was cruel, but because he was incapable of overlooking a lie.

That was why the day I stood before him, carrying a punishment that was not mine, mattered so much. I had done what I believed was right. He believed otherwise.

What happens when loyalty collides with truth, and silence becomes a choice with consequences?

That is a story worth telling.

Chapter 7

BETRAYAL

Major Sandhu was a man of iron – precise, unyielding, incapable of compromise. To be on the wrong side of his principles was every cadet's nightmare. For me, it was unthinkable.

I admired him more than I admitted to anyone. I watched how he spoke, how he stood, how he carried silence as a weapon. In him, I saw the kind of officer I wanted to become – disciplined, respected, beyond reproach. I measured myself against that image every single day.

That was why standing in front of him now felt unreal.

The room was quiet, but the air was heavy. He looked at me, not with disappointment, not with anger, but with something far worse. With certainty. I knew that look well, as I had seen it before, directed at others. Never at me.

Then his voice broke the stillness. "I will ensure you are relegated."

The words landed with finality.

"How dare you submit an incorrect report?" he continued, his gaze never leaving mine. Then he turned sharply towards my Platoon Commander.

"Captain Azimuddin, bring him before the Battalion Commander tomorrow. Prepare a charge sheet. This will be dealt with severely."

Relegation meant losing six months. Stripped of seniority, sent back to join those who had once been my juniors. A quiet erasure.

I stood frozen. Every word felt like a hammer, shattering the image that I had spent years building—not in the eyes of the academy, but in his. My throat went dry. My mind searched desperately for words that refused to come.

I knew the report was wrong. What I didn't yet understand was how the truth had turned into my punishment.

I was a part of the Jessore Company. Amongst the cadets, each platoon was led by a Junior Under Officer (JUO), while each Company was led by a Senior Under Officer (SUO). Just weeks before, I had been appointed as the Junior Under Officer of my platoon. We were in the senior-most term of IMA, about to pass out within the next five months.

The role of JUO was meant to be a badge of honour, a chance to take care of comrades and juniors of the platoon. However, that responsibility came with its share of challenges. One of the challenges was the old barracks where we stayed. These barracks, old and worn from years of use, were in dire need of repairs. And as winter settled over Dehradun, every morning was a gruelling struggle; our washrooms were freezing, and none of the geysers – not a single one of the ten – was working.

I'd tried to discuss this issue with the company's Cadet Quarter Master (CQM), Prashant Rath. The CQM is generally responsible for all administrative and maintenance work. He reports directly to the Company Commander for all issues of administration. But Rath, as competent as he was, was overwhelmed. He was new to the role and, in the beginning, keen on helping. Yet, the weight of his responsibilities started taking a toll somewhere along the line. The urgency he'd once shown in fixing things had faded, buried under an avalanche of other duties.

After days of trying to resolve the geyser issue with CQM Rath, it became clear that he wasn't going to help. Frustration mounting, I decided it was time to take this directly to Capt Azimuddin, my

Platoon Commander. Freshly posted to IMA, Capt Azimuddin was also new to his role and eager to set things right. Our company, Jessore, was also newly-formed, with Maj Sandhu as its inaugural Company Commander. It seemed like the perfect opportunity to get some long-overdue attention to our issue.

Each morning before breakfast, the Junior Under Officers were expected to report to their Platoon Commanders with the day's routine and any pressing issues. I'd resolved to bring up the problem of our unserviceable geysers. The winter chill had settled over Dehradun, and some cadets were visibly struggling. So much so that two of the new cadets had already fallen sick due to the relentless cold.

I was standing in front of my Platoon Commander. After the initial briefing, I decided to take up the case of the geysers. "Sir, I'd like to formally complain about our geysers. They've been non-functional for over a month now," I said, feeling the weight of the cadets depending on me.

Capt Azimuddin looked at me with a slight frown. "I don't recall any complaints about the geysers. The CQM submits a daily report on all faulty equipment to the Company Commander, and I review it regularly. I haven't seen any mention of issues from your platoon."

My stomach sank. "Sir, I've informed the CQM several times about the problem. I've never once told him that everything was in order."

Capt Azimuddin's expression hardened. "Are you suggesting I'm wrong?" he asked, his tone steely.

"No, sir. But I am certain of what I'm saying," I replied, unwavering.

Without another word, he rose from his chair. "All right then, come with me." He strode out of the office, and I followed, my confidence mingling with a touch of anxiety.

In no time, we were standing outside Maj Sandhu's office. Capt Azimuddin knocked, and upon hearing the familiar "Come in," we entered.

"Sir, my JUO here claims the geysers in his platoon haven't been working, though we've received no formal complaints," Capt Azimuddin said, standing at attention.

Maj Sandhu's eyes narrowed, and he reached for a small, well-worn notebook labelled *CQM Report*. He tossed it onto the table in front of me with a flick of his wrist. "Open it," he ordered.

I picked up the notebook, feeling a knot tighten in my stomach. I'd never seen this notebook before, but as I opened it, I saw page after page of meticulously handwritten reports. Each entry contained the daily status updates from every platoon. Then I found the page for my platoon, marked clearly as "No. 8 Platoon." And there, written in careful script, was the statement, *"Everything is working fine in my Platoon. There is no faulty equipment to mention."* followed by a signature – supposedly mine.

My heart sank. I hadn't signed any such report. I'd never even laid eyes on this notebook before today. The realization hit me like a punch. Rath, our CQM, had been fabricating these reports. He'd forged my signature, taking shortcuts to present everything as "fine", while our platoon endured the harsh winter without functioning geysers.

I looked up, meeting Maj Sandhu's unblinking gaze. This wasn't just an oversight; it was outright forgery. Rath had been fooling everyone – and I'd been caught in the middle, risking reprimand for his deception.

"Haven't you signed this?" Maj Sandhu's accusatory voice cut through the room, his eyes locking unwaveringly onto mine.

Panic surged through me. My mind raced as I grappled with the implications. If I revealed Rath's forgery, he would face severe consequences. Forgery is a serious offense in IMA. Rath would face relegation for this charge. If I did that, it would go against the principles taught to us at NDA, which emphasize protecting our comrades, come what may.

Maj Sandhu's frustration was palpable. "Tell me!" he demanded, his voice rising.

I looked down at the notebook, my throat tightening. The weight of my decision pressed heavily on me. Revealing Rath's deceit would uphold the truth, but destroy him. Taking responsibility for his actions would ensure his protection, but it would shatter my career at IMA. At the least, I was sure to be stripped of my appointment as a Junior Under Officer of my Platoon.

"Call CQM," Maj Sandhu ordered, breaking the silence.

I waited for the CQM to come. He should have come and owned up. This was the least I expected from him. Privately, I wanted to beat him to a pulp. He should not have put me in this situation. At least, he should have told me that he was forging my signature. I should have known what report he was giving daily to the Company Commander. Then, I would not have raised the issue with my Platoon Commander.

CQM entered swiftly, his face pale and eyes downcast. The room fell silent, the tension almost tangible. Maj Sandhu wasted no time "Hasn't this JUO been giving you daily reports?" he demanded.

Rath waited for a moment and then said, "Yes, sir." I glanced at him, seeing the fear and regret etched on his face. I looked at him. For a brief moment, his eyes met mine. They were pleading, "Don't tell the Company Commander." I felt angry and helpless at the same time. He should have accepted his mistake, but then I realized he was terrified of the consequences he would have to face.

Maj Sandhu turned his stern gaze to me, holding up the notebook. "Aren't these your signatures?"

I felt a lump form in my throat. The NDA teachings echoed in my mind: *"Stand up for your comrades, never snitch about them, and take punishments if you have to, but always stand by them."* The principles I had internalized over the past three years now confronted me in the harshest way.

'Let me do the right thing,' I thought as I braced myself in front of the man I admired the most.

"Speak up," Maj Sandhu shouted, his voice booming.

I lifted my head and met his gaze. "Yes, sir," I admitted, my voice steady despite the turmoil within me. "These are my signatures."

The room seemed to close in around me as Maj Sandhu processed my confession. "So, you agree that you have been providing misleading reports to the CQM?" he asked, his disappointment palpable.

"Yes, sir," I replied, knowing this admission would anger him further. I stood firm, prepared to face the consequences of my decision.

Maj Sandhu's fury reignited. "I will make sure you get relegated! How dare you give me an incorrect report?" His voice thundered through the room, echoing off the walls.

He turned to Capt Azimuddin without hesitation. "Captain, ensure he's brought before the Battalion Commander tomorrow. And prepare a charge sheet. This needs to be dealt with severely."

As his orders reverberated around me, a surge of conflicting emotions washed over me – fear for my future, sorrow for Rath's predicament, and a deep sense of injustice. I had always strived to embody the values taught at NDA, and today the same principles had brought me to a crossroads where loyalty to my coursemate clashed with the harsh realities of military discipline.

Everything had spiralled out of control that morning. Both my Platoon Commander and Company Commander questioned my integrity, shattering the trust I had painstakingly built. The Company Commander, a man I had always respected and admired, was now condemning me, leaving me feeling utterly betrayed and vulnerable. Instead of merely stripping me of my Junior Under Officer (JUO) appointment, I was to be charge-sheeted for my relegation for six months. This demotion meant I would be junior to my coursemates, setting me back half a year in my career. All this unfolded not because I had failed in my duties, but because I chose to stand up for the principles which the NDA had instilled in me.

I felt utterly dejected. My coursemates offered their sympathies, but their support could only go so far. The following day, I was to be marched up for punishment. CQM Rath didn't dare face me, leaving me to bear the brunt of his deceit alone.

As a disciplined soldier, I braced myself for whatever awaited me. Carefully, I prepared my uniform, the weight of impending disgrace heavy on my shoulders. It was a chilly Saturday morning when I stood resolute outside the office of the Battalion Commander, waiting for my fate.

Minutes felt like hours until the Battalion Staff Officer approached me with a dismissive tone. "Hey JUO, go back to your barracks! The Battalion Commander will not be coming today. Your march up has been postponed until Monday."

Relief was fleeting. The postponement only delayed the inevitable until Monday.

My friends, Sarat and Sandeep, approached me with earnest concern. Their eyes were filled with helplessness as they watched the injustice unfold. Approaching Maj Sandhu had always been daunting; his presence alone commanded silence and fear.

"Go and tell Capt Azimuddin that it was not your fault," they urged.

"There is no way I can tell him anything. Rath would be relegated for sure," I replied, my voice tinged with resignation.

"He deserves that, buddy," Sarat insisted.

"I know, yet I won't do it," I stood firm. It was a matter of standing up for the principles I had always deeply believed in. Though I was disappointed by the CQM's actions, I understood the fear that must have driven him to silence. He didn't come to meet me because he was probably ashamed. I pushed aside my turmoil, but the weight of dejection lingered, sinking me into a deep sorrow.

That evening, football practice was scheduled. As one of the key players, I should have been eager to contribute, but I couldn't bring myself to join. Instead, I chose to sit alone on the grass, the vibrant energy of the field a stark contrast to my inner turmoil.

Unexpectedly, Capt Azimuddin approached me from behind. His presence was commanding, yet his eyes held a hint of concern.

"Why are you not playing, Deep?" he asked softly.

"I'm not feeling well, sir. I need to take a break today," I replied, hoping to deflect his probing.

"There's something wrong that you're not telling me." He pressed gently.

"No, sir," I insisted, my resolve wavering under his sincere gaze.

He studied me for a moment before speaking again. "Okay, come with me. Let's have a cup of tea and snacks in the canteen."

Grateful yet apprehensive, I nodded. "Thank you so much, sir." I couldn't refuse his invitation.

We walked to the canteen, which was eerily quiet. He ordered tea and snacks, the silence between us thick with unspoken questions.

"I know something is bothering you. I know you're not the type to lie. Now tell me," Capt Azimuddin urged, his voice filled with genuine concern.

"Sir, I can't tell you anything," I replied. The repercussions of revealing the truth would be dire for Rath.

"We don't want to do anything wrong, even inadvertently. Therefore, I insist you must tell me."

"Sir, if I tell you, the repercussions will be very bad for someone else," I confessed, the words escaping me reluctantly.

He leaned forward, his eyes earnest. "I promise you that we will not take action against anybody. That's a gentleman's promise."

Desperation and loyalty battled within me. Finally, I found the courage to speak. I told him everything the way it had happened.

Then I added, "Sir, I am an ex-NDA. You are an ex-NDA too. We will never compromise on certain things, and not snitching about our coursemates is one of them. If you act against Rath, then I will not be able to forgive myself."

Capt Azimuddin regarded me silently before replying, "Don't worry. Nothing will happen to Rath." He stood up abruptly. "Let's go back to the football field. Go and play. I don't want you to miss the practice session."

We returned to the football field. The once heavy atmosphere began to lighten, the oppressive tension slowly started melting away as the evening sun cast a cool glow over the freshly-mowed grass.

The dreaded Monday march-up in front of the Battalion Commander never happened. Instead, I found myself standing nervously outside the office of Maj Sandhu in the morning as he approached. My heart pounded in my chest, a mixture of fear and hope swirling within me. He moved closer, his stern expression gradually softening as he regarded me with newfound respect.

"I am proud of you, JUO," he said, his voice steady but filled with genuine admiration. "Your integrity and courage have not gone unnoticed. Now, go back and attend your classes."

A surge of overwhelming relief and joy washed over me. Without a second thought, I sprinted back to the barracks, my legs moving faster than I had ever sprinted.

As I reached my barracks, my coursemates greeted me with encouraging smiles and nods of approval. Sarat and Sandeep clapped me on the back, their eyes reflecting a mix of pride and relief. For the first time in what felt like an eternity, I allowed myself to embrace the moment fully, the weight of the morning's ordeal lifting entirely.

As I walked back to my quarters, the shining sun painted the sky with hues of orange and pink, symbolizing the end of a harrowing chapter and the beginning of a hopeful new day. I felt a deep sense of gratitude for Capt Azimuddin's support and the unwavering principles that guided me through the storm. With my head held high, I knew that no matter what challenges lay ahead, I had the resilience and moral compass to navigate them with honour.

* * *

That day etched a lesson into me that was deeper than any wound ever could. In the Army, honour isn't a slogan; it's a discipline, a code that steadies you even when everything else around you collapses. Betrayal taught me to trust procedures over instincts, integrity over impulse, and to never let emotion cloud judgment in the field.

I walked away from that incident with a renewed respect for the uniform and the responsibility it carried. And as fate would have it, the opportunity to apply every bit of that hard-earned wisdom arrived sooner than I expected. It was during one of the most daring operations I would ever undertake in the Kashmir valley.

Chapter 8

OPERATION SAIDBAKER

November, 1997

I had just taken over as the Team Leader of Bravo Team. The intelligence reports coming in from Poonch and Rajouri were unsettling—whispers of movement, hints of build-up, signs that something was shifting in those rugged mountains. Our team was repositioned from our familiar battlegrounds in the Kashmir Valley to the harsh, forested ridges of Poonch–Rajouri.

But for all the tension in the air, there was nothing concrete to act upon. Not a single piece of actionable intelligence. No confirmed sightings. No intercepts that could anchor a plan.

We had to begin from scratch—conduct our own surveillance, feel the terrain under our boots, study the patterns of life, and identify own targets. But despite the rumours and the restlessness in the air, the year had passed without a single contact with the militants. Not one exchange of fire. Not one shadow that revealed itself.

For soldiers of Special Forces, a dry year is its own kind of torment. The men were restless; the silence felt unnatural. We were waiting—almost hungry—for an opportunity. And somewhere deep inside, we all sensed that when it finally came, it would test everything we had.

* * *

Ten of us moved like shadows up the steep slopes of the Pir Panjal[4] that night. The icy wind tore at our faces, but we pressed on, driven by the silent understanding of what lay ahead. This was a mission into the unknown, where every breath of air seemed to carry the weight of a thousand unspoken dangers.

Majestic Pir Panjal Ranges

The Pir Panjal range, a jagged line of peaks which separated the Jammu region towards the south from the Kashmir valley to the north, had become our new battleground. To the south lay Poonch, Rajouri, and Nowshera – a region that had seen a disturbing rise in militant activity. To the north of the ranges lay Shopian and Pulwama, strongholds of South Kashmir. Poonch and Rajouri had transformed into a simmering cauldron of insurgency.

This mountain range was no longer just a geographic boundary. In 1997, we watched the violence shift from the north to the south. The orders for us were clear – shift focus and our base from the Kashmir valley to Poonch and Rajouri. This sector, once quiet, now pulsed with the threat of hidden foes.

Where the north of Kashmir was lush and dense, South Kashmir lay barren, its rocky face a stark and unforgiving landscape, offering little cover. This stark landscape forced us to rethink our entire approach. The exposed mountains turned every step into a risk, thus making us easy targets under the eyes of hidden observers. The barren mountains made us more vulnerable. Every movement outside our camps felt like being under a spotlight, observed from miles away by those who knew the terrain far better than we did.

And since the local villagers were hostile, that turned the land against us. Their eyes followed our every move, their whispered warnings to the militants echoing through the hills long before we

---

[4] largest and westernmost range of the Lesser Himalayas

could close in. It felt like playing a deadly game of hide-and-seek, with the locals setting the rules. Our patrols and vehicles were like open targets, exposed at every choke point and narrow pass.

Operating in unfamiliar terrain was like groping through darkness. We needed time to map the land's contours, feel its pulse, and recruit local sources who could be trusted with the information. Intelligence was thin, and the enemy was elusive. The more we patrolled these hills, the clearer it became–this fight couldn't be won quickly.

We'd been on the ground for two months, running operation after operation. Most of the operations were without any credible information. We were chasing ghosts. Intel from higher HQ hinted at a large group of militants hiding in these hills, but they stayed out of sight, always one step ahead. This was the early stage of insurgency in Poonch and Rajouri, the time when militants blended in, consolidated, recruited, strengthening their hold. They terrorized the locals, making sure no one dared to betray them.

* * *

Bafliaz

Choosing a location for our camp was a decision that weighed heavily on us. We knew that the success of our operations hinged on our ability to move undetected, yet getting in and out of the camp without drawing attention was a challenge in itself. The surrounding villages were alive with watchful eyes, even in the dead of night, their gaze was fixed on our every move. The locals operated like surveillance posts for the militants, and any hint of our presence or movement would be relayed to them in no time.

That's why we chose Bafliaz as our camp site. Nestled snugly between the hills, it offered a natural shield, allowing us to disappear into the forests and rugged terrain at a moment's notice. Its hidden position also provided a discreet meeting point for our sources, who could come to us without drawing the villagers' suspicions. It was a calculated choice that gave us a tactical advantage, turning the terrain in our favour.

Back in those days, since the information was scarce, we acted on every lead we received, no matter how uncertain. I believed that to truly understand the lay of the land, there was no substitute other than setting foot on it. It was essential to walk the ground, feel its contours under our boots, and map its hidden trails. Knowing that the terrain was the bedrock upon which all our success would be built.

A few hours earlier that morning, we were huddled around a weathered map in our camp at Bafliaz, each of us intently studying the intricate contours and ridges, trying to decipher the intelligence it held. Beside me sat Capt Gaurav Rishi, our Troop Commander, and Dr. (Capt) Akshay Mishra, our Regimental Medical Officer (RMO).

Capt Gaurav's eyes had sparkled with a rare joy when he shared the news of his upcoming engagement. After four gruelling years of relentless counter-militancy operations, his happiness was a beacon of hope amidst the harsh realities that we faced daily. Gaurav had been a key factor in our successes. He had a razor-sharp mind and unwavering dedication, leading the team into various successful missions. Watching him prepare to leave for home the next day filled me with pride and happiness. He often spoke lovingly about Ashima, his fiancée, adding warmth to our otherwise intense environment. We had forged an unbreakable bond through shared hardships, and I was genuinely happy to see him embark on this new chapter of his life.

Across from him, Dr Akshay Mishra exuded a different kind of leadership. Though trained as a doctor, Akshay frequently took on roles beyond his medical duties, thus effectively serving as our team's de facto troop commander. His dream was to move to Australia and specialize further in medicine, a goal that reflected his relentless pursuit of excellence. Yet, it was his infectious smile that genuinely defined him. In the tensest situations, Akshay's positive demeanour could uplift the entire team, reminding us all of the importance of maintaining our humanity even in the darkest of times.

Both of them were busy studying the maps. We were planning the next operation. Military maps were a wealth of information, etched with details that only reveal themselves to those who mastered studying them. Map reading is an art with a language of its own.

Without solid intelligence to rely on, that map was our most reliable guide, revealing hints of the militants' world hidden within its contours. It pointed us towards potential hideouts, outlined the hidden jungle tracks, and marked the locations of water sources such as springs, rivers and streams. It also hinted at possible ambush sites. We studied the positions of villages in relation to the forests, trying to predict the militants' movements, their dependency on villagers for their administration, their patterns, and where they might lay low. In this hostile terrain, the map was the voice of the land, telling us where the next action could be.

Suddenly, the sentry came in, "Sir, Pathan is here. Should I send him in?"

"Please do."

Pathan was a local who regularly provided us with information. Our friendship with Pathan was still new, but we clicked from the start. He had a street-smart edge and an instinct for staying under the radar. I remembered how his father had fallen gravely ill, and he was desperate for money to cover the hospital bills. We had gone out of our way to help him during that crisis, and ever since, a bond of trust had formed between us.

"Hi, *Bhai! Kya khabar?*" I greeted Pathan as he entered, using the local term of endearment that had grown between us. Pathan nodded to everyone in the room before settling in.

"Hill Kaka is getting very active," he said in a low voice, his eyes shifting around as if the walls had ears. "A lot of rations and clothing are being moved there, all bought from the Surankote market. Mules are being used to transport the supplies."

Hill Kaka was a remote village far removed from the urban sprawl of Poonch and Rajouri. No roads led there; the closest motorable track was a two-night walk. Its isolation made it a natural fortress for militants. They could operate without the prying eyes of the security forces in that area. To take on that terrain, we'd need at least three to four hundred soldiers just to manage the logistics and secure the supply lines. The odds were against us.

"Yeah, we're getting similar intel from the Army and police sources as well," Gaurav confirmed, his tone serious.

"There's definitely a build-up happening there," Gaurav continued, his brows furrowed with concern. "It's time we start thinking about pushing into those far-flung areas."

"I agree," I said, nodding. "But before we go in blind, we need to get eyes on that place. Let's set up a surveillance grid to confirm the intel and maybe even get some photos. Then we'll hit them hard, but only when we're ready. Meanwhile, the rest of the team can focus on operations around Surankote."

"Sir, can I stay here for this operation and then go on leave later after we finish this operation? I really want to have a look at Hill Kaka myself. We have been hearing so much about it," Gaurav spontaneously proposed.

"Relax, buddy! Thankfully, someone has agreed to get engaged to you. I want you to focus on your engagement. You must leave for home tomorrow. Don't worry about this place." I snubbed him.

"Let me handle this myself and head towards Hill Kaka," I proposed. "By the time you get back, we'll have the lay of the land, and we can plan our main strike together," I told Gaurav.

"Pathan Bhai, will you join us for this one?" I asked, turning to him.

"Of course, sir. Just say when," Pathan replied without hesitation.

"Tonight, by last light," I said. "I don't want to waste a moment. Rest up, Pathan Bhai. Be ready to move."

I felt a surge of adrenaline at the thought of leaving under the cover of darkness. The moon was in its third quarter. It would be dark when we would start casting just enough shadow to shroud our movements as we slipped past the villages. By the time the bright moonlight flooded the hills, we'd be well into higher ground, where we could move faster under its silver glow.

It would take us two nights of trekking to even come close to Hill Kaka, and somewhere along the way, we'd need a hiding spot, a "harbour" in our tactical jargon. I'd already marked a potential harbour on the map, nestled off the beaten path where we could lay low during the day. Moving in daylight would be a death wish; we'd use that time to rest and regroup, conserving our energy for the final push.

After Pathan left, I turned to Gaurav and Akshay. "I'll be taking the route through Said Baker. I would have to be clear of that place by first light. If I get stuck there during daylight, we'll be trapped in the valley with those hills watching our every move. My first aim is to cross Said Baker before dawn."

"There's another problem, sir," Akshay said, his face tense. "Our Nursing Assistant (NA) is on leave. The replacement we have got doesn't look like he could handle a jog, let alone this trek."

I sighed. "We need the NA with us for such a deep operation. What's the option, Akshay?"

"I'll come with you, if needed," Akshay offered. There was no hesitation in his voice. Akshay was more than just a doctor; he was a warrior in his own right. The top of his batch from Armed Forces Medical College (AFMC), he had courage stitched into his very being. He had saved countless lives on the battlefield, going where bullets flew and where the wounded cried out for help.

"I'll need you here as the reserve, Akshay. With Gaurav on leave, you're our only backup," I said, meeting his steady gaze. "We'll take the new NA. He might be dead weight, but we don't have the luxury to be choosy."

"Yeah, I forgot to mention that the CO will arrive tonight from Udhampur. Akshay, please receive him while I am away," I instructed, my voice steady despite the day's mounting pressures. Col Britto, our Commanding Officer, had already set out from Udhampur and was expected to reach Bafliaz by late evening. His visits were not very rare, yet always impactful, serving as a much-needed boost to our team's morale.

Akshay nodded. He concurred that these visits were more than just formalities; they were moments of reassurance and unity that reminded us why we endured the relentless challenges of our missions.

I glanced around the map-filled room, feeling a pang of anticipation. I wanted to speak with Col Britto, share my thoughts, and seek his guidance on our upcoming operation. His leadership was a pillar of strength for us, I mused, hoping that we could meet once I returned. The thought of discussing our strategies with him filled me with a sense of confidence and calm amidst the chaos.

* * *

Delta Post, Kupwara
Preparing for an Operation

In Lolab Valley,
with our Tracker dog – Rocky.

Combat Shooting:
Eyes open, Double tap, Counting rounds.

Operation at Hill Kaka, 2001.
With Maj *(later Col)* R.S. Gill and others.

Moments before Operation Dardpora—
with Team officers.

Day harbour in thick jungles.
Resting by day, Movement only at night

On the heights
of mighty Pir Panjal ranges.

Combat shooting practice in Haphruda forest during time at base.

With a dear friend and commando buddy, Capt *(later Col)* Hemanto Panging, Kupwara.

After a long operation, a cup of tea and a moment to rest is all you neec

The Balidan badge
an elite insignia of the Indian Army's Parachute Regiment (Special Forces).

Paratrooper Surya Prakash:
The sunlight of the Bravo team.

Capt Deep Bhagat,
Instructor, Class 'C',
Commando School, Belgaum (1999).

Practicing snake handling skills
at Commando Wing, Belgaum.

Skydiving at Sarsawa,
Saharanpur, 1998.

Commanding the battalion at Shamshabari Range,
Line of Control, with my pet Buzo, 2007.

Army Day Parade, 1999
Tea hosted after the investiture ceremony where I was awarded the Sena Medal *(Gallantry)*, with my parents, COAS Gen V. P. Malik, and Maj Sudhir Walia (ADC).

With my four-year-old nephew Captain Abhinav,

With my family
—my wife, parents, uncle, and Abhinav, during the investiture ceremony, Delhi, 1999.

The last picture before hanging my uniform.
Deep, Charu, Anish and Akshaj.

The Climb

We'd been climbing for over two hours, our breath ragged and visible in the cold night air. Pushkar, our scout, led the way with practiced silence, his eyes scanning the shadows ahead. I followed closely, every muscle tense, my senses heightened for any flicker of movement or rustle in the dark. Pathan was right behind me, his presence like a shadow at my back, while the remaining seven men trailed in a single file. Naik Dharam Pal brought up the rear. His role was crucial–guarding our backs, ensuring that no one lagged or got lost in the darkness that swallowed us whole.

We'd managed to slip out of our camp as planned, melting into the hillside under the cloak of night. So far, the silent villages below seemed unaware of our departure, but that comfort was temporary. The real challenge was just beginning.

It was November, and the harvested maize fields lay barren, their terraced slopes exposed under the moon's unforgiving light. As the moon climbed higher, our cover would dissolve into thin air, and we'd be visible to any watchful eyes that were perched on those distant village rooftops. We had to cross this first line of villages before the moon turned us into easy targets.

Suddenly, Naik Dharam Pal approached, his face a mask of concern. He whispered, "Sir, the new Nursing Assistant isn't doing well. Stomach cramps. We might need to halt."

A spike of irritation shot through me. This was not the time for weakness. "For how long?" I asked, forcing my voice to stay even though inside, I was seething.

"Just a moment," Dharam Pal said, but I could sense the doubt in his tone.

I made my way to the NA, who was crouched on the ground, clutching his midsection in pain. "What's going on?" I demanded; my voice as cold as the wind cutting through the mountains.

"Stomach pain, sir. I can't walk," he gasped, his face twisted with discomfort.

"You don't have a choice," I said, my words sharp and unforgiving. "We're racing against the dawn here. If we don't move now, we'll be sitting ducks by first light. Get up, or we leave you behind."

The NA's eyes widened, fear mixing with determination. "Give me a moment, sir. I'll manage," he forced out, struggling to get to his feet.

"Make it quick," I muttered, doubt gnawing at me. Had I made a mistake by bringing this man along? Was this the weak link that would compromise the entire operation? Minutes were slipping away like sand through my fingers, and with each passing second, the sky grew a shade lighter. My mind raced. We needed to clear Said Baker's ridgeline before dawn, or this mission would collapse before it even started.

We waited for ten minutes. I nervously waited for the NA to respond. Another precious ten minutes passed. Just when I was on the verge of pulling the plug, the NA gritted his teeth, straightened, and looked me in the eye. "I'm ready, sir," he said, trembling but resolved.

"Are you sure?" I asked, knowing full well that hesitation was a luxury we couldn't afford, even though I wished I hadn't asked that question at this dire moment.

He nodded, his jaw clenched tight. It wasn't confidence, but it was enough to move on.

"All right, men," I said, my voice low but urgent. "We've lost time and need to make up for it. Double the pace. We have to hit Said Baker before dawn, or we turn to ghosts in these hills."

As we started moving again, I turned to Pathan, my voice barely a whisper. "How much farther to cross Said Baker?"

"Not far now," Pathan replied, his voice calm, yet unwavering. "We'll make it before first light."

His words were steady, but I knew the terrain ahead was anything but forgiving. My survival instincts screamed at me to keep pushing harder, faster. The darkness was our ally now, but the moment the first rays of sunlight touched those hills, we would be exposed. We pressed on, our steps quickening, every sound amplified in the stillness, as if the mountains were listening to our every move.

I felt the chill of the cold November night and of time slipping away. The stakes were too high, and I knew there was no room for error.

The terrain was unforgiving – high-altitude ridges and sparse settlements. We knew we were approaching a *dhok*, a small, dark dwelling used by locals and often by militants, as a resting place. Pathan whispered, "This one's at a crossroads. Militants often stop here when they cross over from Pakistan."

"Could they be there now?"

"Not sure, sir. I just know they use it."

I paused, stopped the patrol, and moved back to meet Dharam Pal.

"What do you think?" I asked Dharam Pal. "Should we check it or press on?"

"At this time, we have no confirmation about anyone in this dhok. Checking without any input will not be an intelligent decision. Not only will we waste time, but we will have to abandon this operation, sir," he reasoned.

"Agreed. But stay sharp. We'll skirt it from the rear," I said to Pushkar, my lead scout.

The dhok was still some distance away, its outline barely visible under the pale moonlight. Pushkar moved with heightened caution, every step deliberate. I followed close behind, my rifle poised and ready. We had barely taken fifty more steps when a faint sound reached us. A soft "*thukk*," the unmistakable snap of a twig breaking. It came from the direction of the dhok. Pushkar and I exchanged a sharp glance, both freezing in place. That sound didn't belong here; there was no reason for it in the dead of night. It was a warning, clear as day. Someone else was out there.

Without a word, we burst into action. Pushkar veered to the right flank, where the door of the dhok was, while I leaped onto the mud roof in one swift motion from the left flank. In that split second, I spotted them– a group of figures darting out of the dhok, their shapes stark against the moonlit snow. Militants, no doubt.

Chaos erupted in front of us. The door of the dhok flew open, slamming against the wall as men poured out in a frantic rush. They moved as a pack, turning sharply to the left, sprinting towards the cover of the hill's curve. The moonlight flooded the scene, illuminating the snow on the upper ridges and casting a bright, unforgiving glow on the ground below.

With the maize fields now barren, the militants were visible as they bolted through the open terrain. The gap to the turning at the spur was barely 25 metres. We had seconds to act. Because, if they reached that corner, they'd slip into the darkness. They had to be stopped before they disappeared into the shadows

I flipped my rifle's safety to fire, braced, and squeezed the trigger, firing rapidly, but with precision, aiming for centre mass. I counted each round, one after the other. Twenty shots, and I ducked to reload as Ravinder, my buddy, joined me and laid down suppressive fire.

Then everything went still.

I took out my rucksack and crouched behind it, my heart pounding. Did I get any of them? The moon cast long shadows, pitch black beyond ten metres. I strained my eyes, looking for any sign, but the darkness swallowed everything. Suddenly, Ravinder tapped my shoulder. "Sir, we need to fall back. They might regroup and counter-attack."

Just as we began to reposition, a grenade blast shook the ground near the door, followed by a burst of automatic fire. Boom! Rut-a-tat-a-tat!

"There's still one inside the dhok!" I shouted. "He's firing from the door and window. We can't let him escape."

We quickly regrouped and surrounded the dhok, taking up defensive positions. Close-quarter fighting in the darkness was every soldier's nightmare – confusion, shadows, and split-second decisions where one mistake could be fatal. If he made a run for it, we had to be ready.

We still had no confirmation about the militants who had earlier run out into the night. Whether they were wounded, dead, or regrouping somewhere beyond the ridgeline was unknown. But one fact was now certain: a militant was still holed up inside the dhok. And whatever the cost, he could not be allowed to slip away under the cover of darkness.

I glanced at the chimney on the roof. An idea struck me. I could drop a grenade down and end this. I moved quickly, pulling a grenade from my vest and preparing to toss it. I closed in on the chimney with a grenade in my hand.

Just then, I heard a child's cry from inside through the chimney.

I froze. A cold wave washed over me. Civilians! A family. "Damn it!" I muttered under my breath, heart pounding. One second later, and I'd have been responsible for something unforgivable.

The darkness of the night hung heavy around us, but my heart lightened with gratitude. "Thank God I heard the child crying," I murmured to myself. "Otherwise, I would have thrown the grenade inside." I could only thank divine intervention for saving me from a dreadful mistake. But as relief flooded my veins, a pang of frustration followed. The terrorist inside had also escaped a sure death. If I had thrown that grenade, he would have been finished. *Maybe I could still fire through the chimney*, I thought.

Gripping my rifle, I aimed it into the black void of the chimney and squeezed off two rounds. I wasn't expecting much. Maybe nothing would happen, but at least I tried. Either way, I was relieved to have avoided sinning today.

The firing from inside the dhok ceased. Two possibilities crossed my mind – either the terrorist had already slipped away under the cover of darkness, or he had resigned himself to his fate, planning to fight again come morning. Regardless, we'd have to wait until dawn.

The first light was three hours away, and an eerie calm settled over the battlefield. The silence felt tense. Apparently, the terrorist inside was conserving ammunition for the morning assault. I had time now, so I decided to check in with my Commanding Officer (CO) on my radio set, who had reached Bafliaz after I had left for the operation.

I took out my radio set and called "Five Zero for Nine Five. Over." Nine Five was the CO's call sign.

"Nine Five for Five Zero, Come on. Over," came the crackling reply. Col Britto was waiting for my call. The shots had been heard in the camp, where Col Britto was still awake and having a chat with Capt Akshay.

"Contact established with terrorists at 2:30 a.m. No own casualty. Results not confirmed. One terrorist holed up inside the dhok. Over."

"Great! You take care. Is there anything required from this side? Over," the CO asked.

"We'll need ammunition for the Rocket Launcher and some more men. Over," I replied. The danger was far from over, and I wanted to ensure we were well-prepared for tomorrow's operation.

"Roger! Captain Akshay will reach you by first light with the required ammunition. Call me if you require anything else. Nothing else. Out." Nine Five hung up.

I looked forward to seeing Capt Akshay. But right now, all eyes were on the morning ahead. I made the rounds, checking on my men and ensuring every escape route from the dhok was covered. Finally, Ravinder and I settled into our positions.

Dawn broke slowly, revealing the field inch by inch. I strained my eyes, searching for the bodies of the terrorists. My reputation as a sharpshooter—and, more importantly, as a Special Forces officer—was on the line. As the light spread, I spotted them. Two bodies lay sprawled in the open field. Two terrorists were down.

Great! So far, so good, I thought.

I ordered Dilip and his buddy to sweep the area before we attempted to clear the dhok. Whoever was left inside could wait. Our safety came first. By now, Akshay had reached our location with reinforcements and supplies.

Suddenly, Dilip's voice cut through the morning air. "Sir, come here fast! I see another terrorist lying ahead!"

I sprinted over, my heart pounding in my chest. There, lying face-up with his legs toward me, was a burly man with long, curly hair. I thought he was dead. Suddenly, his eyes snapped open as I approached, and his hand twitched towards me. He was holding a pistol in his hand. And then he fired at me.

Tap! Tap!

Two bullets whizzed past my head. He was trying to sit up to get a better aim. His shots missed, but my rifle didn't. I took a breath, steadied my rifle, and fired a headshot. His skull exploded, but I wasn't taking any chances. I dashed around him, making sure he was indeed dead.

That was the third terrorist down. Now, the dhok remained.

Back at the dhok, my men were still in position, ensuring no one slipped out. *First things first*, I thought. *We must get the civilians out.*

I shouted, "Everyone inside, please come out! No one will harm you."

A tense moment passed, and then the door creaked open. My men, weapons trained on the entrance, waited for any sudden moves. A middle-aged man emerged; hands raised. What followed shocked me – one woman and seven children came out with him.

"Oh my God! Seven children!" My knees nearly buckled with the realization. "I wouldn't have forgiven myself if I had thrown the grenade through the chimney." I silently thanked God a hundred times. That mistake would have haunted me forever.

They walked towards me, hands still in the air. I called the man over. "What's your name?"

"Hussain," he answered, his voice shaky.

"How many terrorists are inside?" I demanded.

"No one. I swear," Hussain replied, but I wasn't buying it. The terrorists hadn't likely escaped; we'd been guarding the dhok all night. Still, there was a slim chance.

"Okay, then come with me. We'll both go inside and check your dhok," I said, taking Hussain by the arm. We cautiously entered. A weapon gleamed on the floor. Instinctively, I fired. A dead terrorist lay there, his fallen AK-47 glinting in the dim light. His burly frame and tactical gear indicated he was someone of significance, likely a commander. I fired a couple more rounds just to ensure that he was down for good.

Turning to Hussain, I seethed, "You said no one was inside! You lied!"

I ordered Hussain to pull the terrorist out, but as he grabbed the legs, a metallic clink echoed. It was the unmistakable sound of a grenade pin. Time slowed to a crawl.

One thousand one, one thousand two… I mentally counted as I dragged Hussain out with me.

One thousand four… BOOM! The grenades generally took four seconds to blast. That is all the time one has to evade an injury. When it's a matter of life and death, this time is sufficient.

The explosion rocked the dhok, dust and debris flying everywhere. We'd made it out by a hair's breadth. My heart hammered in my chest.

I hauled Hussain aside, away from his family. "Tell me what's happening! How is that man dead with a grenade in his hand? If you're hiding something, I swear I'll kill you," I threatened, my patience wearing thin.

"Sir, I am a poor man. The terrorists come and stay here at their will. I can't do anything. They're dangerous, but fair to us. They pay for food and tea," he pleaded.

"Okay. Tell me what happened today."

"Sir, there were five men. Three of them were foreign mercenaries. They had a meeting. One went to urinate outside when he saw your men approaching our dhok. He panicked and ran back to warn the others. Most ran without even putting on their shoes. The group leader, Abu Bakr, was still wearing his shoes when your firing began. He couldn't get out and stayed inside," Hussain explained.

His story matched up. I realized the first "thuk" sound we'd heard must have been that man who had come out to urinate.

Hussain continued, "Abu Bakr tried to fire through the window and door. He was about to throw a grenade when two shots came down the chimney. He was standing right underneath it. Both bullets hit his head. The grenade stayed clutched in his hand. When we moved him now, the grenade fell out of his hand and exploded."

The mystery unravelled in front of me, dotted with coincidences. The Nursing Assistant's delay meant that we arrived just when one of the militants happened to be outside to urinate. We might have moved on without realizing it, had they all been inside. My shots through the chimney killed Abu Bakr purely by chance.

We had neutralized four terrorists in a fast-paced, close-quarter engagement. The fifth had managed to escape into the surrounding villages. He was later found dead by the locals, a single bullet lodged in his jaw.

Wounded and hiding, he had tried to make his way towards Surankote for medical help. But by then, all approach routes had been sealed. With no access to a hospital and no possibility of evacuation, he bled out in the shadows, far from the firefight that had begun his end.

When we finally reached Bafliaz, my CO, Col Britto, was there to greet us.

"Congratulations, buddy. Well done! Ask me for anything, and it's yours." Generally, we never saw the CO excited. This was a welcome change. I didn't want to miss this opportunity.

"Allow me to meet Charu in Udhampur, sir. Our anniversary is two days away. It's our fourth year, and we've never celebrated one together," I said, thinking of my wife.

"Granted. You are a smart guy." Col Britto's smile was as wide as mine.

"Thank you, sir."

Charu would be so surprised. She never expected such miracles to happen in 9 Para. The thought of seeing her brought a rare smile to my face, and my men noticed it. They knew what a victory it was! Not just against the enemy, but against fate itself.

The terrorist group we had originally set out to hunt in Hill Kaka would live to see a few more days. Their time would come soon enough, I thought, leaning back in my Jonga as it bumped along the road to Udhampur.

The Said Baker encounter changed something in me. It was a reminder of how thin the line is between decision and disaster, life and death.

On 15th January, 1999, Army Day, I was presented the Sena Medal for this operation by the then Chief of the Army Staff (COAS), General VP Malik, during the morning parade in Delhi. The honour felt less like a personal achievement and more like a tribute to the men who stood with me that night. I was grateful, humbled, and more thrilled than I can admit.

But the celebrations didn't end there! The same evening, the award winners were invited to the COAS House for tea. I thought it would be a simple, formal event. I had no idea that a small family "operation" was waiting for me. It turned out to be far more unpredictable, amusing, and memorable than *what* I had faced in Said Baker.

Chapter 9

OPERATION TEA PARTY: Gallantry Award & a Four-year-old Captain

January, 1999

This was, without doubt, one of the happiest days of my life. It was 15th January, 1999 – Army Day. I had just been presented a gallantry award by the Chief of the Army Staff (COAS) during the morning parade. My chest felt like it might burst from pride. I'd dedicated my life to serving my country, and now I was being honoured for it in front of my peers, my family, and the nation's top leaders.

As part of the celebrations, all award recipients were invited to the COAS House for the evening tea. It was already a momentous occasion – meeting the Chief of the Army Staff on such an illustrious day, but the VIP guest list took it to an entirely new level. The President of India was going to be there, along with the then Prime Minister, Mr Atal Behari Vajpayee, and various ministers and opposition leaders. This was a formal affair, with strict invitation protocols.

The adventure began much before the tea party had even started. Having just received the gallantry award, I should have been the most relaxed man in Delhi. But instead, I found myself planning a covert operation to smuggle my parents and my four-year-old nephew Abhinav into one of the most high-security gatherings in the capital. Compared to the enemy-infested mountains of Kashmir, this mission was supposed to be simple. Little did I know that the real test of the day wasn't the medal; it was keeping Abhinav's excitement under control.

Officially, each awardee was permitted to bring only one set of guests—either a spouse or parents. That was where my dilemma began. My wife was with me in Delhi. My parents had travelled all the way from Lucknow to share this milestone. And to add to the complexity, my four-year-old nephew, Abhinav—my sister Priya's elder son—had tagged along. The instructions were unambiguous: children were allowed only if they were the sole child of the couple.

My mother was overjoyed. She had long admired Mr Vajpayee and could scarcely believe she might meet him in person. Watching her excitement, I knew there was no way I could deny her that moment. And yet, one after another, the problems stacked up.

First, the rules allowed either the spouse or the parents—not both. Second, I already had three adults in tow. And finally, there was Abhinav—a lively, curious, four-year-old missile—determined to be part of the action. Leaving him alone in an unfamiliar place was out of the question. Crushing my mother's dream was unthinkable.

Somewhere between protocol, family expectations, and a child brimming with excitement, I realized that this evening demanded more ingenuity than many operations I had conducted in uniform.

I racked my brain for a way to sneak everyone past the entry gate. Then I remembered: Captain Sudhir Walia, an officer from my own unit, was the ADC (Aide-de-Camp) to the COAS. If anyone could orchestrate a covert mission to bring my family in, he was the man for the job. Thankfully, he understood my plight, and in true Army-buddy fashion, agreed to help me. Perhaps it was bending the rules just a bit, but after everything we'd done together in the service, this felt like a small favour.

The plan was simple, but not exactly fool-proof:

1. My mother and father would accompany us as if they both had permission. Captain Walia would be present at the gate to take them through.
2. Abhinav would come along with my wife and me, pretending to be our son.

The presence of a four-year-old at such an event was bound to attract attention. We needed a fool-proof identity cover. Our solution? A battlefield promotion.

That night, we drilled Abhinav like a recruit in training. I knelt to his level and said, "Listen, buddy. Whenever someone asks your name, just say, 'I am Captain Abhinav.'"

He nodded enthusiastically, his big eyes sparkling with excitement. I repeated, more firmly this time: "I say again, buddy – by no means should you say you're Abhinav Mukherjee."

My sister had married into a Bengali family, and if he blurted out his real name, I'd surely be in trouble. So would Captain Walia. I wanted to be absolutely sure that Abhinav wouldn't slip up, even inadvertently.

The stakes were high for me, but for Abhinav, everything was fun. He giggled and nodded.

My heart pounded when we approached the entry. I wasn't nearly as nervous about receiving a gallantry award as I was about smuggling my parents and nephew into this high-profile gathering. One suspicious glance from security, and we'd be caught. But fortune favoured us – Captain Walia intercepted us at just the right moment, replied to my salute, and nodded us through.

Mission accomplished. The COAS House was abuzz with energy, teeming with top Army officers, cabinet ministers, and esteemed guests. I was trying to keep Abhinav's hyperactive curiosity under control. Four-year-olds aren't exactly known for their restraint, after all.

Soon, the Prime Minister entered, graciously greeting everyone in his path. Standing next to me, my mother fell silent the instant she saw him. For a woman who was otherwise unshakeable, it was surreal to watch her freeze in sheer awe. Mr Vajpayee paused, noticing her reverent gaze, and offered his trademark gentle smile.

I nudged my mother softly. "Mom," I whispered, "Please say something! This is your big chance to talk to the Prime Minister!"

She managed only a breathless "Namaste," hands folded in respect. Mr Vajpayee nodded, clearly touched by her sincerity. In that moment, I felt an overwhelming surge of gratitude for my family's support, for the Army that shaped my life, and for the once-in-a-lifetime chance to see my parents brimming with joy and pride.

I can't remember a time I felt happier or more fulfilled. Seeing my mother, usually so strong and confident, transform into a little girl meeting her hero was priceless. And knowing that my father stood quietly by, looking at me with pride, made my heart swell. The mischief of sneaking them in suddenly felt justified, the kind of story I knew we would laugh about years later.

The grandeur of the place was overwhelming. The lush green lawns were dotted with decorated soldiers, top generals, and the political titans of the country. Here I was, standing shoulder-to-shoulder with the men and women I had only seen in newspapers and on television.

We listened to Dr APJ Abdul Kalam, the Scientific Advisor to the Prime Minister, narrate stories of India's missile program and future technological advancements. The way he spoke, with an almost childlike enthusiasm, made even the most complex scientific ideas sound like bedtime stories. At that moment, I was a fan, a listener, a student absorbing the greatness of these people.

But I never let Abhinav out of my sight. The little guy was my ticking time bomb. One wrong answer, and our grand mission would crumble.

And then… disaster struck!

From the corner of my eye, I spotted Mr KR Narayanan, the President of India, walking towards us with Gen VP Malik. I panicked.

Before I could think of an escape route, they were right in front of us.

Mr Narayanan's gaze landed on Abhinav, who was standing there looking adorable in his little outfit. The President bent down, smiled, and shook his tiny hand.

Before I could react, Gen Malik spoke up, assuming what seemed obvious. "He is Major Deep Bhagat's son."

I let out a silent sigh of relief. Maybe we had dodged the bullet. But then came the real test.

The President looked directly at Abhinav and asked, "What's your name, beta?"

I swear, I skipped at least three heartbeats. I could feel sweat forming under my uniform.

Abhinav, to my utter horror, paused. *No, no, no! Not now, buddy! We practiced this!*

He looked up at me with the most innocent, mischievous eyes, as if savouring the moment.

Then, in the most confident voice ever, he said, "I am... Captain Abhinav." He stopped and glanced up at me again, a victorious glint in his eyes.

I could almost hear his silent message, "Calm down, Mama. Don't think I'm a kid. I got this."

The President chuckled. "Wow! Wow!" He patted Abhinav's

head. "I am sure you are going to be an Army officer one day, like your father."

At that moment, I wanted to hug the little genius. Not only had he saved us, but he had also won over the President of the country.

I let out the biggest breath of relief.

For the rest of the evening, I watched Abhinav bask in his newfound rank and admiration. Dignitaries smiled at him, officers ruffled his hair, and he proudly strutted around the tea party like he actually was a young Captain in the Army.

As we left that evening, I realized that, while gallantry medals and military honours are priceless, this little adventure was something I would treasure forever.

Years later, when Abhinav grew up, we often joked about his first "field mission" in disguise. I would tell him, "Not many people get to meet the President of India as a four-year-old officer."

And he would grin and reply, "Not many uncles get to pull off such crazy infiltration missions either."

* * *

As the gates of the COAS House closed behind us, the noise of Delhi lingered for a moment longer than it should have. Abhinav's laughter, polished shoes on stone, the soft weight of pride sitting on my shoulders.

Moments like these had a strange aftertaste. They stayed with you, even when you tried to move on.

And move on, I did.

Because somewhere far from the manicured lawns and ceremonial salutes, the Haphruda forests were waiting. The kind of place that did not care who you were in Delhi, only how quietly you moved and how well you listened.

Chapter 10

LATERAL THINKING

May, 1998
Camp Kakrosa, Haphruda, Rajwar

Seated in the cramped office of the Team Commander at our Company Operating Base at Kakrosa, the air was thick with anticipation as we sipped tea in silence. The calm was shattered when the door flew open, and in strode Altaf, his face flushed with urgency, eyes alive with a glint of excitement.

"Sir, I've got big news!" he said, barely catching his breath. "A new group has just crossed over from Pakistan." His words carried a weight that was impossible to ignore.

I fought to keep my face steady, suppressing the spark of adrenaline. "Take a seat, Altaf," I replied, my voice level, almost too calm. "Let's hear the details."

Altaf's words tumbled out in a rush, but I listened with a practiced stillness. I'd learned long ago that in this game, excitement clouds judgment. The devil always lurks in the details, and missing even one could turn the hunter into the hunted.

Ilaqa-e-Rajwar

We were operating in one of the most dangerous regions imaginable – Rajwar. It was a rugged area in the Kupwara district which is part of North Kashmir. At the heart of Rajwar lay the dense forest of Haphruda, a place that breathed danger with every gust of wind that rustled through its thick canopy. Its tangled undergrowth and towering trees created a labyrinth where visibility was limited, and every shadow felt like it was hiding a threat. A long list of soldiers killed in action is attributed to fighting in the Haphruda forest.

Haphruda was the gateway for militants crossing over from Pakistan. Being the closest forest to the Line of Control (LoC), it was the perfect staging ground for infiltration. For these incoming groups, Haphruda was their first stop. They used it to regroup, rest, and plan their next move. They stayed hidden in its depths, waiting for the right moment to disperse into other parts of Kashmir, their paths carefully laid out by their handlers.

This forest was hostile terrain and a stronghold for those who sought to slip through our defences. For us, it was a place where every step felt like a confrontation with the unknown, where the stakes were as high as the silence that seemed to swallow us whole.

In the world of counterinsurgency operations, intelligence is our lifeline. Simply put, information is power. But that power is fragile, coming mostly from human sources that could be as unreliable as they were valuable. Trust was the hardest currency in these mountains, and the stakes were always life or death.

I remembered how different things were two years ago, when Haphruda was a fortress for militants – a dark, impenetrable forest that had devoured many brave souls who dared to step into its shadows. Back then, the militants' grip on the villagers was unbreakable. No one dared to whisper a word to us, let alone hand over information.

Winning Hearts and Minds

Three years ago, as a young troop leader of my team, I had stood in these very villages, feeling the weight of their hostile eyes on me. To them, we were the enemy, outsiders in their land. That day, I had sworn to myself that one day, I would infiltrate more than just militant territory. I would get into the hearts of these people.

I had realized then that the real battleground wasn't just hidden in the dense forests or the rugged hills. It lay in the hearts and minds of the villagers. The day they chose to speak to us freely, without fear or hesitation, would be the day we would truly have gained ground against the militants. I knew that was our turning point, the key to shifting the balance. So, I made it my mission, almost an obsession, to earn their trust, to win them over, one person at a time.

To do that, our entire approach had to change. We needed to strip away the hard edges, the combat-ready exterior which we wore like armour. We had to be friendlier and more open and ensure that any aggression we held towards the militants never showed in front of the villagers. It was vital that they saw the difference between us and the threat we were fighting.

This was no easy task for us; we were soldiers, trained to fight, not to befriend. Our interactions with the villagers had always been limited, and trust didn't come naturally in such a hostile environment. But I knew that if we wanted to break through this wall of silence, we had to start with ourselves. We needed to be more than just uniformed men; we needed to be human, approachable, and willing to listen.

I decided to press forward with my mission to break the ice. It was clear to me that true success lay on the other side of their fear and mistrust. And I was certain that if we could bridge that gap, we could turn the tide in this silent war. I had to believe that once we reached them, once they let us in, everything would change.

Slowly, the ice began to thaw. Suspicion turned into curiosity and then into cautious trust. Some villagers even started feeding us information in whispers behind closed doors. My intelligence network grew, but I never let my guard down. Every piece of information was still a double-edged sword – helpful, if true; deadly, if false.

As Altaf finished his hurried report, I leaned back and narrowed my eyes, weighing his words. Even now, I knew the truth could be hidden beneath layers of deception, and every lead had to be stripped down, examined, and war-gamed before we could make a move. In this shadow war, acting too fast could mean falling into an ambush set by our haste.

"Good work, Altaf," I said finally, a hint of a smile playing at the corners of my lips. "But now, let's peel back every layer of this intel before we make our move. Remember, one false step, and we're not hunting them—they're hunting us."

We all sat over our map, and Altaf started again, "Sir, they crossed over near Tangdhar yesterday. They're likely to pass through Hagnikut in the next four hours, heading towards Woysa and then Kaonar," Altaf said, his eyes gleaming with excitement. "The intel is solid. This is our chance!"

Facing Phantoms

Altaf's energy was contagious, but I kept my expression neutral, my mind running through calculations. The militants he spoke of had breached the Line of Control and were heading straight into our area of operations. The route he mentioned was delightfully close to our camp. Woysa village lay just two kilometres to the South, with Hagnikut to its West and Kaonar to its East – a tight cluster of terrain that offered both opportunity and risk.

It was 12 noon, and we had just enough time to set up our ambushes on this route in the hope of catching the militants off guard. But the real challenge wasn't whether we had enough time; it was how to move without tipping off the enemy to our presence. The militants were clever in how they planned their movements. They would usually choose to travel between noon and evening, a tactical choice which was based on caution and calculation. At that time of day, they could be almost certain that no Army patrols were hiding nearby or sweeping the area. They knew that if the Army was going to lay any ambushes, it would already be done by then. So, once the militants had confirmed that the coast was clear in the afternoon, they would feel confident enough to move during the remaining daylight hours.

But their confidence didn't just come from their own observations; it was reinforced by their network of villagers acting as their eyes and ears. These villagers kept a close watch on our camp and any Army patrols that left it. They'd relay this information in real time to the militants, ensuring that the militants had live updates on our movements. This allowed them to make calculated decisions, knowing exactly when and where they could pass through safely. That's why the militants often chose to cross the area closest to our camp before darkness fell. They trusted that their local informants would have spotted any Army presence by then.

I was studying the map intently, looking for a possible route to intercept these militants.

"Altaf, four hours might be enough to lay ambushes between Woysa and Kaonar," I said, leaning forward, "but how do we get to those ambush sites without tipping them off?"

This was like a chess match played in the shadows, and the militants always seemed to have the upper hand. They had two powerful advantages that tilted the scales in their favour – intelligence on our movements and a deep understanding of the terrain.

In these villages, the militants were like phantoms that lived among the people. Most villagers were too scared to defy them, and many preferred to stay in the militants' good graces. For the villagers, helping militants often meant protection or even rewards in the form of cash and favours.

The militants had woven a web of informants, an invisible network that spanned the entire valley. It was a silent communication line that worked faster than any of our radios. The moment an Army patrol left the camp, the word was out, and the militants were gone before we even knew they were there. It was like we were always chasing shadows.

To complicate things further, some local boys from these villages were drawn to the militants. This was partly out of fear and partly because they idolized them. To these young men, the militants represented power, rebellion, and a kind of swagger that came with carrying a weapon. They were born in these hills; they knew every trail, every cave, every hiding spot like the back of their hand. When these locals teamed up with foreign mercenaries, who were battle-hardened guerrilla fighters who had spent years in conflict zones, it created a deadly blend of knowledge and experience.

The militants could slip out of any trap we set, blending into the landscape, led by the local boys who knew the terrain intimately. They didn't just know the ground; they owned it in a way that every engagement on their turf felt like we were walking into an ambush.

As Altaf briefed me on the routes, I scanned the map. Hagnikut to Woysa. Woysa to Kaonar. It wasn't far. We knew the area well, since we had been operating here for quite some time now. I had ambush locations in mind that would surely trap the militants. But we'd be noticed the moment we set foot outside our camp; villagers would send word, and the militants would vanish like smoke. By the time we'd settle into our ambush, they'd either change course or delay their movements, slipping through our fingers once again.

This was the challenge of Kashmir. The ground we walked on was hostile, while the shadows watched us constantly. We were battling the very ground beneath our feet, the villages that stood in silence, and the whispers that travelled faster than our bullets. In this environment, the odds were always against us.

But I wasn't ready to let this opportunity slip.

Something had to be done. The conventional plan wouldn't work. I had to think of something else to reach the ambush location. Something out of the box. *What should I do? How could we reach the ambush sites by remaining invisible in this broad daylight? God! I wish I knew some trick to make me invisible.*

Idea!

Suddenly, a plan formed in my mind; a way to turn the villagers' tactics against them. I called for my senior JCO, Roshan Sahab, who was a seasoned soldier. He was a world-class skydiver and a true professional, the kind of leader who kept the entire team on their toes. His level of preparation was unmatched. Thanks to his discipline and meticulous planning, we were always ready to move out of camp at a moment's notice, day or night.

"Roshan Sahab, gather the men. We roll out in ten minutes. Also, send Capt Anil Malik to me right away," I ordered.

Capt Malik arrived swiftly, his face lit with the raw eagerness that only a freshly minted officer from the IMA has. Though new to the unit, he was sharp, brimming with energy, and itching to prove himself. I knew that in this new scheme, his role would be crucial. He was relatively unknown to the villagers, which gave us a tactical advantage. Today, he'd be leading the ambush teams while I would serve as the decoy.

"Listen Anil," I said, locking eyes with him, my tone urgent. "We've got intel on a group crossing from Hagnikut today. I need you to form three ambush parties – four men each, lightly equipped and ready to stay for the night. We move in ten minutes. You'll be the point man on this one. I'll be using myself as a distraction to keep the villagers' eyes off you. Make sure your teams are invisible out there."

Anil's eyes gleamed with determination as he saluted with a sharp nod. "Understood, sir. We'll be ready," he replied, already turning to get his men into action.

I threw on my combat gear—my AK, three rifle magazines, two grenades, a radio set, extra batteries, a medical kit, and, oddly enough, a bag of chocolates and toffees. I knew the importance of blending in and sometimes the most minor details mattered the most.

* * *

The Plan

The plan was simple in concept, but required precise execution. We organized three ambush teams, of four men each, strategically positioned to blend seamlessly into a larger patrol unit. For this operation, we mobilized everyone that we could – cooks, washermen, and every available man on the camp roster. I needed a large patrol that would stretch across at least a kilometre, making it nearly impossible for the villagers to accurately estimate our numbers.

The idea was to create a sense of unpredictability. The larger the patrol, the harder it would be for anyone watching to figure out where our real strength lay. Hidden within this extended line of men, the three ambush teams would move quietly, ready to split off at just the right moment.

As we advanced towards the target area, the plan was for these ambush teams under Capt Anil Malik to discreetly peel off one by one, each settling into pre-designated spots. We had to make sure that they were not watched when they quietly slid inside the jungles. They would set up their ambushes silently while the main patrol would continue its route towards Woysa village, maintaining the illusion of a routine patrol. This way, anyone observing our movements would believe that the patrol was just another standard security sweep.

Once the ambush teams were in position, the larger patrol would turn back and return to the camp, leaving the militants unaware that traps had now been set in their path.

However, the real challenge wasn't in the planning, but in the execution. Moving such a large group in broad daylight came with its own risks. Every step we took was scrutinized by unseen eyes. Daylight movement meant that the element of surprise was slipping through our fingers, making it difficult to execute the split without drawing attention. We knew that even a small mistake could turn the ambushers into the ambushed.

The stakes were high, and the terrain was unforgiving, but this was the gamble we had to take. In this deadly game of hide-and-seek, we had to make the enemy believe that they were watching our every move while our real intent remained hidden in plain sight.

The Ambush

We moved in a staggered formation. As many as 75 men stretched out along a column so long that by the time our leading scouts reached Woysa, the last soldier hadn't even left the camp. Each man kept a 50-metre gap from the one ahead, a deliberate spacing that turned our patrol into a silent puzzle for anyone observing us. They could see us moving, but with those distances, it was nearly impossible to gauge our true numbers.

Daylight made every step we took more exposed, so maintaining that distance was more than just a tactic; it was a lifeline. If an ambush were to come, no two men would be caught in the same burst of gunfire. This formation wasn't just about spreading out; it was also about survival in the face of uncertainty.

I led the way, not as an imposing figure, but as a familiar visitor to the village. With a bag of chocolates in my hand, I walked into Woysa with a smile, more like a guest than a military officer. The villagers knew me; they recognized the face of the man who led these soldiers. And in their minds, where I went, the centre of the action followed. This would work for us as Capt Anil Malik would be free to peel off when the time came. No one would watch him.

As we approached Woysa, children playing cricket on the outskirts ran up, curious. I dropped my rucksack, pulled out the toffees, and handed them out with a smile, engaging in small talk with the villagers. They watched me closely, suspicious but unsure. I knew the drill. By now, word of our movement would have reached the militants. But they were about to miscalculate.

While I kept the villagers distracted, Capt Anil Malik and his three ambush teams melted away into the surrounding forest, slipping into the shadows like ghosts. The militants wouldn't know they were there.

Fifteen minutes later, my radio crackled to life with the coded message: "Ambushes are in position." A wave of satisfaction washed over me as I bid farewell to the villagers, turning back towards the camp with a casual demeanour. The children waved at us, blissfully unaware of the trap that had just been set. To the villagers, it looked like any other day – a routine patrol that came, handed out chocolates, and left without incident.

The stage was now set. The militants, convinced that the area was clear, would walk straight into the trap laid by Capt Malik and his teams. Now, the success of our plan hinged on one crucial factor: the accuracy of our intelligence. I hoped with every fibre of my being that the information we had received was spot-on.

But another worry gnawed at me – an uncertainty that always lingered in operations like these. Had anyone spotted Capt Malik's teams as they moved into their positions? If even a single pair of eyes had seen them, our entire plan could be compromised.

To safeguard against this risk, I made a quick decision. I shifted my position from the front of the patrol to its rear while on our way back to the camp, taking a small team of five men with me. I wanted to be closer to where the action would unfold, ready to respond in an instant if something went wrong. This way, I could reach Capt Malik's location as soon as possible if his teams found themselves in trouble. The ambush was set; now, we had to rely on precision, patience, and a lot of luck.

Climax

As evening descended and the shadows stretched long across the landscape, the militants began their movements. Confident and without hesitation, they advanced, believing the Army had withdrawn. But these militants were seasoned fighters; they knew better than to move as one large group, especially when a high-ranking commander was among them. They sent two young scouts ahead as a vanguard, a tactic that kept their main force out of immediate danger.

These scouts led the way, cutting through the forest trails while the rest of the group followed at a cautious distance. This way, if there was an ambush, the scouts would bear the brunt of it, thereby allowing the main party to either evade or counterattack. It was a strategy born out of hard-earned experience in guerrilla warfare.

The scouts approached the first ambush position. Both scouts moved very cautiously, one behind the other. Capt Malik had the first scout in his sights, his rifle steady, every muscle in his body tensed for action. But he hesitated, realizing that these two weren't the primary targets; they were merely the advance party, a decoy to probe for danger ahead. Like us, they were using tactics to feel out the enemy's position before exposing their core strength.

Malik found himself in a dilemma, caught in the razor-thin moment between action and restraint. Should he open fire on these two scouts and risk alerting the main group, or should he wait, gambling on the chance that the rest of the militants would soon come into his kill zone? The decision wasn't easy. His mind raced through the possibilities. If he fired now, he could eliminate the scouts, but might lose the opportunity to take down the commander and the main force. If he held back, he risked the entire ambush unravelling. "Nothing doing," he finally decided, his instincts taking over. "A bird in hand is better than two in the bush."

He knew the risks. Darkness was creeping in, and if he didn't act soon, the entire group might slip away, leaving them empty-handed. He had to strike while he had a clear shot.

The stillness of the jungle shattered with the sharp crack of gunfire. The first scout fell on the ground. The bullet had pierced his head. The second one jumped to his right, making it into the thick undergrowth.

The Chase and the Close Call

The moment the first shot echoed through the jungle, I was already in motion, adrenaline surging through my veins like wildfire. Grabbing my five men, we sprinted towards the ambush site, every muscle tuned to the urgency of the chase. We moved with the swiftness of a shadow, knowing we had a narrow window before the dense forest devoured all traces of the fleeing militant.

After ten minutes of breathless pursuit, we reached the ambush site. The ground was littered with the aftermath. One body of the dead militant sprawled awkwardly, his rifle partly hidden in the underbrush. Capt Malik crouched nearby, his eyes fixed on the darkening tree line, alert and tense.

"One slipped through, sir. He vanished into that stream," Malik said, pointing towards a thicket of dense foliage. "He wouldn't have gone far."

It was 5:30 pm, and in this part of the country, the night would descend in another half an hour, turning our world into a shadowy trap. Searching in the dark was dangerous; it was a perfect scenario for the hunter to become the hunted. The militant had every advantage now—concealment, the element of surprise, and an intimate knowledge of the terrain. He could be lying in wait, his rifle trained on us, ready to ambush anyone who dared to approach.

I felt the weight of the decision pressing on me. Common sense urged me to pull back, to regroup before darkness closed in, but my gut said otherwise. The thought of letting this militant slip away gnawed at me, and I couldn't shake it.

"We've only got half an hour of light," I said, gathering Malik and the NCOs in a tight circle. "Do we pull back to safety or take a calculated risk to flush this guy out before he escapes?"

The dilemma was palpable. On one side was the safety of my men, a responsibility I couldn't take lightly. On the other was the burning desire to deal another blow to the militants, to capitalize on the moment. The faces around me were tense, their eyes darting from me to the jungle as they weighed the risks.

"Fifteen minutes," I said, cutting through the silence with a voice that brooked no argument. "We'll search for fifteen minutes. If we find him, we finish this. If not, we pull back immediately. No unnecessary risks."

My eagerness must have shown. The men looked at me, nodded, and we moved.

Our scouts moved ahead, taking point as usual, but this time, I positioned myself right behind the lead scout. I needed to be close to the action. We crept into the undergrowth, a stream glistening to our left, bordered by low hillocks that could hide a dozen threats. The jungle closed in around us, each branch clawing at our uniforms like skeletal hands, the air thick with tension.

The tactic was straightforward but brutally effective: We fired intermittent shots into the bushes, trying to force the militant to reveal his position. If he were there, he'd either have to shoot back or shift his location, and any movement would betray him.

We advanced in slow, deliberate steps, each of us taking turns to spray bullets into the foliage. The forest swallowed the noise, echoing it back in eerie silence. My rifle was angled to the right, covering that sector of the jungle. I was second in line, with Vilas right behind me, his eyes sweeping our flanks.

Time stretched thin, seconds turning into minutes, each heartbeat like the tick of a countdown. The jungle refused to give up its secrets until Vilas shouted with urgency

"Sahab! Banda, *bayen ko, gyarah baje*!" (Sir, there's a man! Eleven o'clock, to the left!)

His clarity in indicating the target was razor-sharp. Vilas used the clock-ray method—our shared language in chaos. If our direction of advance was twelve o'clock, eleven meant just off the left shoulder, forward of us. Without thinking, I swung my rifle to the left and fired in the direction he pointed. Two shots. The militant must be somewhere there.

Tap! Tap!

And then suddenly, my rifle clicked empty. A dead, hollow sound that sent a chill up my spine. My blood froze. I'd been firing continuously, unaware that my magazine held only two rounds. Now I stood there, exposed, weapon silent, the militant still out there – alive or dying, I couldn't tell – and for a fraction of a second, I was the most vulnerable man in the jungle.

In that split second, everything seemed to slow down. My breath, my heartbeat, even the rustling of leaves around me. I was out of ammo, standing wide open in the crosshairs of an enemy I couldn't see. Reloading would take at least five long, dangerous seconds…an eternity in combat. My fingers fumbled for another magazine, but I could already feel the weight of my mistake settling in. One mistake that could cost me my life and the lives of my men.

I was learning the lesson of my life: *Always count your rounds in the magazine. Always.*

I dropped to a crouch, instincts kicking in as I took a new magazine out of my combat vest. Meanwhile, Vilas stepped up, his rifle spitting fire. In those precious seconds, he covered me; his rounds found the militant, silencing him before he could fire back.

As I reloaded, the lesson hit home hard: *In combat, complacency kills.* I had to be sharper and more prepared. Every round, every second mattered. You couldn't afford to be caught off guard, not in these moments where life and death danced so closely.

Lesson Learned

We had succeeded, but the price was a humbling one. Our lateral thinking had got us to the ambush locations, yet I realized that combat doesn't care about rank or experience; it only cares about who's ready in the heat of the moment. I realized then that no matter how much I thought I was prepared, there would always be variables, always contingencies which I wouldn't have planned for.

But I grew up learning this: *Even if you lose the battle, you do not lose the lesson.*

'Fall, you must, but rise again, wiser each time.'

Haphruda ended the way every soldier hopes an operation will end – objectives achieved, men accounted for, ground quietly handed back to the mountains.

Success has a way of lowering your shoulders, if only for a moment.

But in our world, the next mission never waits for the dust to settle. Even as one operation closed cleanly, another began to take shape – smaller, quieter, and far less forgiving. It was an intelligence task. Routine on paper.

It would change everything.

Chapter 11

SURYA PRAKASH—THE SUNLIGHT OF BRAVO TEAM

Honouring fallen comrade: Paratrooper Surya Prakash
June, 1998

June arrived with its own storms. The confidence earned from our previous operation hadn't dulled my caution, but it did give me a sense of readiness as we stepped into a remote village under a moonless sky. Still, something about that night felt different. The darkness pressed closer, every sound sharper, every breath heavier. And before dawn broke, we would come face to face with a tragedy that would forever change the story of our team, and of Surya Prakash.

* * *

I found Surya Prakash lying on the mud floor of the verandah, his breath coming in harsh, uneven spurts. His buddy had managed to drag him out of the firefight zone, bringing him to the safety of the village shop's verandah. The air around us was too silent. The only sound was his laboured breathing, and for a moment, I felt a flicker of relief. At least he was still breathing.

A dark, suffocating blanket covered the village. Not a single light flickered in any house, as though the ghosts of the place had swallowed them. In hindsight, I understood: the militants' movements must have been constant, forcing the villagers to stay hidden in the pitch-black night, too scared to risk drawing attention.

The new moon didn't dare show itself. In the combat zones I'd grown up in, I'd learned the moon's role in our operations. On full moon nights, everything was illuminated, leaving no shadows to hide in. During the new moon, like tonight, the world vanished into absolute darkness, with only the faintest glimmer of starlight piercing through. Such nights were the most dangerous. Tonight, even the stars were shrouded by thick clouds. The trees stood like silent sentinels, their shadows stretching into the unknown.

The stillness was the deceptive calm after a firestorm. Surya Prakash had been hit. A bullet to the head. I resisted the urge to check his injury; shining a torch could give us away. The danger was real. The militants who had attacked us could still be lurking nearby, waiting.

We were a five-man team on a high-stakes information-gathering mission in a remote village, hidden deep in the hills. The area was crawling with militants. Night operations were always risky, but the stakes were even higher now. Identification was key. If you fire too soon, you risked hitting innocents. Hesitate, and you could end up in a firefight with no room for mistakes.

* * *

Information about militants was crucial for any successful operation. My source had passed on word that one militant was attempting to surrender. He was holed up in a village north of our Company position. A month ago, he'd slipped through one of our ambushes. Now, disillusioned, he was ready to lay down his arms. If true, he could be an invaluable asset, a source of real-time intelligence. And more importantly, he was willing to talk. The temptation to act was almost too great to resist.

But we couldn't afford to rush in recklessly. To stay concealed, we needed complete darkness. The new moon night was perfect—no light to betray our movements. It would give us the cover to closely observe the militant's house ensuring we weren't walking into a trap.

Such missions always carried risks. It could be a trap, an ambush designed to lure us into the open. But sometimes, you have to take those chances.

As the Team Commander, I led the information-gathering missions. It was a role I relished. It played to my strengths, letting me meet new people and piece together the puzzle of human nature. I thrived on cerebral challenges.

For this mission, I had handpicked five men. Surya Prakash, my No. 2 scout, was with me, along with Hav Randhir, my lead scout. The area was unfamiliar. We had never set foot in this village. Navigating off the map, we were entering unknown territory.

By midnight, we had reached the village. My informer led us straight to the target house, a large, ominous structure cloaked in darkness. The perimetre was marked by a wooden fence, with only two doors flanking either side of the house. We held our positions, watching from the shadows for nearly an hour. Once we were certain there were no signs of movement, we made our move.

Out of the five of us, three stayed outside, guarding the perimetre. Two of us, along with our informer, slipped through the wooden fence and into the grounds. The remaining men remained stationed on the southern side, keeping watch over the T-junction. Surya Prakash was assigned to cover the eastern approach.

What Surya didn't know was that just five metres ahead, the track he was covering veered sharply. That was where the militants emerged from three of them, rifles drawn and ready. They moved swiftly, scanning every inch of the path. Nothing would go unnoticed. They had only one mission – to neutralize any threat. And Surya, who was only five metres away, was in their sight.

Surya heard them before he saw them. His mind raced: Shoot, or don't shoot? Were these villagers? But Surya, despite his limited time in service, had matured quickly. No shots without confirmation. He would never risk hitting an innocent.

In that split second of hesitation, Surya switched on his Night Vision Goggles (NVG) and raised them to his eyes. The faintest flicker of light from the goggles, barely perceptible, betrayed his position. The militants were too quick. They unleashed a burst of automatic fire, retreating behind the turn from where they had come. Surya was caught in the open, barely five metres away. The bullets found their mark.

In our line of work, we'd learned one truth all too well: *Light is death.* The tiniest glimmer from the NVG's lens was enough to put Surya in their crosshairs.

I was tens of metres away, crouched in the darkness, listening intently to my informer's words when I heard a burst of automatic fire, sharp and relentless. It was uncharacteristic of Special Forces, who prided themselves on precision-firing and single shots. The sound was enough to send a jolt of dread through me. It meant the militants had taken the initiative. They had fired first.

My heart sank. I sprinted towards the firefight, hurdled over the fence, and reached Surya Prakash, who was already on the ground. Meanwhile, the rest of the team engaged the retreating militants, trying to keep them on the run.

As my fingers brushed his head, a cold, chilling liquid soaked into my hands. I didn't need to confirm it. I knew – either blood or the grey matter from his brain. The thought of it struck me like a blow to the chest. In the suffocating darkness, I couldn't tell if the bullet had gone deep or just grazed his forehead. But one thing was certain – Surya Prakash was still breathing, though his breaths came in erratic, laboured gasps.

I refused to accept it. As a diehard optimist, the thought of anyone dying in my arms was simply impossible. Not on my watch. Not in my team. Surya had to survive. He *would* survive. For four years, I'd fought in the valley, and no one had died under my command. I clung to that belief. I was the favourite son of god, after all. I had saved every man, and I would save Surya, too.

Without hesitation, I reached for my rucksack, grabbing the IV bottles from my first-aid kit. The conditions were less than ideal. The night was pitch black, and I had to shield the torchlight while I searched for his veins. The seconds felt like hours. His heart rate was dropping too fast, and I could feel the veins retreating with every passing second. Despite the chill in the air, I was drenched in sweat, my hands trembling, but there was no time for doubt.

I was desperate to save Surya Prakash. He was the youngest paratrooper in my team, barely 19 years old. He had joined us just a year ago, during our operations in the Rajouri-Poonch area. I could still hear the words of our Commanding Officer, clear as day, during his visit: "Deep, look at his age! We were chasing pretty girls at that age, and this kid is chasing militants." I couldn't help but nod, agreeing with him completely. It was as if fate had carved out a different path for each of us—one that had led Surya into the heart of danger.

Tonight, that same young soldier was fighting for his life. His breath was coming in uneven, rattling gasps, and each one unsettled me further. I couldn't stand the thought of losing him. "Stay with me, buddy," I urged, my voice tight with emotion. "I will not let anything happen to you. I'm getting you to the hospital."

For a brief moment, he squeezed my hand. The gesture, so simple yet profound, sparked a flicker of hope. It was the lifeline I needed. I couldn't afford to waste a second. My mind raced through evacuation plans, getting him to the road where a Jonga would take him straight to the Field hospital in Kupwara. I quickly unbuckled his belt, removed his shoes. I needed him to breathe easier, to find some comfort, even in the midst of all this chaos. We'd carry him to safety, whatever it took.

* * *

The drive through the crumbling roads took an eternity – an hour and a half of relentless urgency, with nothing on my mind, but getting Surya to the hospital. Every second counted. Every breath he took seemed like a prayer. Panting and exhausted, we finally arrived, hauling Surya straight to the doctor, who was already waiting in the main lobby.

I could barely choke out the words. "Save him, doctor!" I pleaded, my voice cracking with desperation.

The doctor didn't waste any time. He examined Surya, his face grim. "Sorry, Major," he said, his voice flat. "But he's dead."

I couldn't accept it. I couldn't hear those words. "No," I cried, my heart breaking. "He's still breathing. Look at him. You *have* to save him." My mind refused to let go, but my emotions threatened to drown all reason.

The doctor shook his head, his expression hardening. "He's clinically alive, buddy. But look at the grey matter everywhere. He's gone."

The words hit me like a blow to the chest. Nothing in life had prepared me for this. The tension, the adrenaline of the last few hours, had all been building to this moment. And when it hit, I couldn't hold it back. Tears… tears I didn't know I had left, poured down my face uncontrollably. I sobbed, not caring who saw. It was the first time in my life that I felt this kind of loss.

Just then, a fellow Commando pulled me aside. "Sahab, please wipe your tears. The entire team is watching. You cannot show weakness now."

His words hit me like a cold wave. My mind, still reeling from the loss, couldn't grasp the wisdom of his words, but I obeyed mechanically. I wiped my tears, the grief still suffocating me. My conviction to save Surya had been shattered in an instant, but I knew the mission had to go on.

That year was 1998.

Years passed, and despite my fierce desire to visit Surya Prakash's home in Shimla, the demands of my professional life kept me from making that personal journey. The memories of him, however, never faded.

* * *

Finally, in 2009, my wife and I decided to make the trip. I reached out to fellow unit members, who met us in Shimla and helped arrange our visit to Surya's house. It was a one-hour drive through the winding roads, and the closer we got, the heavier my heart felt. Surya's parents, brother, and sister-in-law greeted us with warmth and grace. His sister-in-law brought a framed picture of Surya, and for a moment, I found myself staring at that young face, once so full of life, now frozen in time. He had been like a kid to me, and that frame, with his smiling face, struck me deeper than I had expected.

As I stood there, lost in memories, Surya's niece ran into the room, her laughter a sharp contrast to the heaviness in the air. She ran towards us, her innocence bright and playful. And then, in a moment that felt like a punch to the gut, Surya's brother revealed something that would haunt me forever – their daughter had been born on the exact same day that Surya died. The tragic coincidence hit me hard. Surya's mortal remains had returned to this home on the same day his niece arrived from the hospital. In their grief, Surya's family embraced their daughter as an incarnation of Surya, a living reminder of the boy they lost.

As I looked at her, that young girl full of life, emotions surged within me. I couldn't hold them back any longer. Tears welled up, threatening to spill over. I couldn't speak, couldn't do anything except look at the daughter who had somehow filled the space that Surya had left behind.

* * *

In the aftermath of Surya's death, as a form of symbolic revenge, every time our team eliminated militants from Harkat-ul-Ansar Tanzeem, we named the operations after him – *Operation Sunlight I*, *Operation Sunlight II*, and the series continued. The three militants responsible for Surya's death came from the same group, and each operation felt like a silent tribute, a way of honouring him by striking at the heart of those who had taken him from us.

Even now, in the shadows of that harrowing night, my heart still sinks when I think of Surya. The memory of him—the young, eager soldier who never had the chance to live out his potential—remains etched in my mind.

Surya's death left an emptiness which no tribute could ever truly fill. Yet even in my grief, I was reminded of a truth I had learned again and again in Rajwar and Haphruda: no soldier fights alone.

In that brutal, unforgiving terrain, saving lives demanded tactics, trust, delicate handling of locals, and respect for the fragile human networks that hold the valley together. I didn't know it then, but one of the pillars of that network—the man who would change our operations forever—was waiting for me in the thick forests of Haphruda. His name was Chacha.

Chapter 12

CHACHA: THE UNSUNG HERO

August, 1998

Charu lay alone on her bed in the hospital ward.

It was her second miscarriage in three years. I was not there, yet again.

She had undergone an emergency procedure after another ectopic pregnancy. The fertilized egg had ruptured inside her fallopian tube. She had lost consciousness. By the time I heard the full truth, the danger was already past. But at that moment, she was alone, broken, and waiting for me.

And I was deep inside Kashmir.

Fate had placed my team in Rajwar, in the jungles of Haphruda – dark, unforgiving terrain close to the Pakistan border. Thick forests, hostile villages, and a steady flow of foreign militants had turned this belt into one of the most violent places on earth. Haphruda did not forgive mistakes. It consumed men quietly and without ceremony.

That day, a message came from my Commanding Officer.

"Reach back to Udhampur immediately."

No explanation followed. None was needed.

Something inside me collapsed. I knew this was about Charu. No one in Udhampur told what had happened. Perhaps they thought silence would help me focus. It didn't. It only made the dread heavier. I knew this was the moment she needed me the most. She would never say it aloud, but the truth was unmistakable.

For five years, Charu had been my strength, my quiet, uncomplaining powerhouse. She had stood alone through absences and fear. She had carried the emotional cost of my profession without ever making it my burden.

I realized then that I had been postponing something inevitable. It was time to go home and the timing could not have been worse.

Almost simultaneously, tragedy struck my professional family. Chacha – our long-time associate, our informer, the man who had stood between us and death for three relentless years – had been abducted. Foreign militants had taken him from his home. He was tortured and butchered. His family was left defenceless, ostracised by the village, marked forever.

Two lives.

Two loyalties.

Both demanding me at the same time.

Yet, the decision was clear.

Charu needed me now. More than the Valley. More than the mission. More than my uniform.

A new team commander, Major Panging had taken over Kakrosa. I briefed him, shook hands, and drove out in my Army Jonga. As I passed through the market, I saw them.

Rashid and Feroza ji stood at the crossroads.

Feroza ji held a baby girl in her arms. Rashid clutched the hand of another. They didn't wave. They didn't speak. They simply stared at me.

Their eyes said everything words could not.

Don't go.

They were Chacha's family.

For three years, I had met them in fragments of darkness – short, cautious visits that were meant to protect Chacha's identity.

Now, they stood exposed, abandoned, and afraid. I drove past them, knowing I was leaving them behind.

That image still haunts me.

It was in 1995, when I had come to Haphruda for the first time. In a fierce encounter, we had eliminated five militants. It became immediately clear that this place was infested, mostly with foreign mercenaries. But, eliminating militants without credible local intelligence was impossible.

Someone had to get us the information. That was when Altaf, a close associate in the Valley, introduced me to Chacha.

Our first meeting was clandestine; under the cover of night, far from curious eyes. Chacha was desperate. His wife was critically ill. He had no money for her treatment. For him, survival had narrowed down to a single, dangerous choice.

For me, it was the beginning of everything.

If intelligence had to take root in Haphruda, it had to begin here. With him.

I just needed to look after him and make sure that he didn't get exposed. Through him I would get other villagers on my side, who could start supporting me. I was confident that once I taste success in eliminating militants, more people would support me. But, it had to start from somewhere. Therefore, Chacha was extremely important.

To protect Chacha, our visits to his house were rare and brief. There could be no routine, no familiarity, no visible pattern. We moved only in the deepest hours of night, when the world slept, and fear relaxed its grip for a few precious moments. We would listen, clarify, cross-check, and leave.

But those fleeting meetings were priceless. In those stolen hours, Chacha unfolded Haphruda for us, layer by layer. He spoke of newly-infiltrated groups, subtle shifts in militant hierarchies, fractures and rivalries between tanzeems that outsiders could never detect. He knew who had arrived, who had fallen out of favour, who was recruiting, and who was consolidating. He explained how civilians were coerced, sometimes with money, sometimes with ideology, often with fear.

This was not raw information. This was *processed intelligence.*

Chacha had an instinct for reading the land and its people. He absorbed fragments from conversations, movements, silences, and stitched them together into a coherent picture. I wanted to meet him more often, to extract every ounce of his understanding, but restraint was survival. Every meeting increased his risk. I had to constantly balance my hunger for intelligence with my responsibility for his life.

What made this bond extraordinary was that Chacha was never alone in this endeavour. His family stood firmly behind him.

Rashid and Firoza ji were not passive bystanders. They listened, observed, and supported him quietly and resolutely. During our visits, they would prepare mutton and naan for us, served without ceremony but with immense warmth. As members of the Gujar-Bakharwal mountain tribe, hospitality was part of their identity. But here, it went far beyond custom. Every meal they served us carried risk, and yet they never hesitated.

Within the first month, the gamble began to pay off. Acting on Chacha's inputs, we apprehended a dreaded Lashkar-e-Taiba militant in broad daylight. The shockwaves were immediate. Within a week, two more militants were eliminated. For the first time, I sensed movement—something shifting in Haphruda's hardened ground.

Those initial successes were crucial. We were operating under immense pressure. There was no safety net, no alternative source, no second chance. We had to succeed quickly to establish credibility, yet patiently to avoid exposure. It was a razor's edge.

And Chacha held that balance with us.

As our confidence grew, so did the trust of others. Within six months, two or three more locals quietly stepped forward. Some went as far as carrying radio sets, risking instant execution if discovered, so they could alert us about militant movements in real time.

That six-month period changed everything.

What began with one man, driven initially by desperation and later by belief, became the foundation of a living intelligence network. Haphruda did not open itself to us because of force or fear. It opened because Chacha chose trust, and his family chose to stand beside him.

Everything that followed—every success, every operation, every dent we made in that militant stronghold—was built on those first anxious months. On one man's courage.

One afternoon, we received information on our receiver radio set. One militant had come to a local house to meet his girlfriend. Seeing an opportunity, we swiftly moved our teams to the location and eliminated him. He was Samundar Khan, an IED expert. This was a major jolt to the militant leadership.

Friendship with Chacha was leading to fruition. I had to make sure that no information about Chacha was leaked out. He had to be saved at any cost. In this war of shadows, the safety of an informer is of extreme importance. You lose one source, you lose all sources. Our credibility was at stake. And so were our battles in one of the most violent places on earth.

But at the same time, militants were furious. They knew that if they did not hold the local population with an iron hand, it was just a matter of time before all of them would be eliminated.

They started hunting for anyone who was giving out their information. They were sure that people were providing information to the security forces. They had to nip the problem in the bud before it grew more menacing. They had aggressively started looking for the informer.

Finally, our luck ran out after three years of intense operations in Haphruda. Suspicion had fallen upon Chacha as an informant of the security forces. Disaster struck us abruptly. On one of the most heart-wrenching nights for Chacha and his family, the terrorists arrived at his house in the night and abducted him. Most of them were foreign terrorists. By the time information about his abduction reached us, it was way too late. Chacha was taken to an unknown location. The terrorists took all the time in the world to torture the old man and executed him brutally, making an example out of him for the entire village.

We were shattered. Execution of a 'source' is bad news anyway. Chacha's demise was a disaster. Our credibility had taken a beating. I was furious, but helpless. Chacha's family was left devastated, and their own community ostracized them for helping us. The family was very dear to me, and I wanted to do everything possible for them in this time of need.

It was at this time that I received the message from my Commanding Officer. I was in Haphruda thinking about Chacha and his family. Though no details were provided by the Battalion Headquarters at Udhampur, I came to know from a close friend that Charu had undergone her second miscarriage.

I had to depart immediately. My departure from the valley was heartrending. Yet, duty to my own family and an ailing spouse remained paramount for me.

As I departed in my Army Jonga, my thoughts lingered on Rashid and Firoza ji. Their future loomed uncertain, overshadowed by poverty and a hostile environment. The legacy of Chacha's heroism seemed destined to fade, a story known only to a few. I was one of the last to have lived that era.

In 2008, my work brought me back to the Valley, where I had witnessed my trials and triumphs. Time had moved forward, and with the advent of technology, staying connected had become more feasible. As I stepped back into the embrace of the valley, I reconnected with Chacha's family. Their unwavering support during times of peril had etched an indelible mark on my heart.

The passage of years hadn't diluted the connection; rather, it had strengthened it. A sense of responsibility enveloped me, propelling me to embrace the role of a guardian for the family that I held dear. I enabled the children's education through financial support, sowing the seeds of empowerment. After completing high school, the eldest daughter ventured into the tailoring business. She was the one who had stood on the crossroads of Kakrosa holding Rashid's hand. Yet, it was the second daughter who illuminated the path. She was the one who was in Firoza ji's lap. With unyielding determination, she now pursues her MA in Political Science from Ganderbal, Srinagar. Two younger brothers, who were born later are still pursuing their studies.

For me, it wasn't merely an act of generosity, but a profound debt repaid. The family that had risked everything to support our mission was deserving of every ounce of assistance which I could provide. My career journey took me across lands, but my bond with the family remained unwavering. Our connection has thrived over the past twenty-six years, nurtured by a commitment that knew no physical boundaries.

In September 2022, the wheels of change propelled me on a motorcycle odyssey–a journey of nearly 2500 kilometres from Pune to Kupwara. This distance paled in comparison to the emotional reunion it heralded. Col Prithvi Chauhan, a veteran and a dear friend accompanied me on this voyage of heart and soul, joined by officers from the Special Forces team currently serving in the region. The culmination was a heart-warming reunion with the family. The Kashmiri people are renowned for their hospitality; we witnessed it at full display that day. I was very happy to meet the younger daughter, who had travelled all the way from Ganderbal to meet me. The elder daughter was set to marry in just one month. She looked radiant with excitement, and I couldn't have been happier for her.

A serene panorama unfolded as I stood amidst the tranquillity of the village. The once-troubled region had transformed into a tapestry of hope. Roads now stretched to the farthest corners, breathing life into every village. Haphruda, once a violent and bloody battleground, now stood on the brink of metamorphosis into another Gulmarg, with beautiful meadows that had been converted into resorts and ski slopes. I saw the change that we had always dreamt of. People were thriving. They were happy. Peace was back in the Valley. I knew this change was due to the efforts of the very people that I had come to meet.

As I look back on a journey that has stretched across decades, I am struck not by regret, but by responsibility. When I visited Chacha's home again, I saw the familiar struggles – an uncertain livelihood, winters that still bite hard, debts that refuse to loosen their grip. Life had not been kind or fair to his family. Yet, what I saw more clearly than hardship was resilience.

They had endured without bitterness. Without complaint.

That is when I understood something Chacha had taught me without ever articulating it – dignity does not come from comfort or security, but rather from choice. Chacha chose courage in a world which was ruled by fear. His family chose loyalty in a time of betrayal. And together, they proved that even the smallest human connection can tilt the balance of history.

Soldiers like us often stand in the spotlight, our actions recorded and remembered. But behind every successful operation, some men remain invisible—men who carry no weapons, wear no uniform, and yet shoulder risks greater than ours. Their information saves lives. Their silence protects missions. Their courage builds the foundations on which victories are raised.

Haphruda was such a place. A land that gave birth to heroes, and quietly took them away. Chacha was one of them.

What endures, however, is not how he died, but how he lived—and what he set in motion. The intelligence network that we built, the successes that followed, the peace that slowly returned to the Valley—all traces back to one man who chose to trust, and one family that chose to stand beside him.

If I continue to stand by them today, it is not out of obligation or sympathy. It is out of gratitude. A debt willingly carried, not because it must be repaid, but because it deserves to be honoured.

In the end, wars are not won by weapons alone. They are won by relationships. And sometimes, the bravest soldier in the room is the one history will never name—but whose courage makes every other act possible.

Chacha's death pulled me backwards in time. Loss has a way of doing that. It awakens memories you thought had settled, wounds you believed had scarred over. As I stood grappling with what Chacha and his family had given and lost, I found my thoughts returning to another home I had once visited, years earlier, under very different circumstances.

That journey had been in mourning, too.

It was then that the memory of Captain Arun Singh Jasrotia returned – not as history, but as a presence. His sacrifice had taken place years before, yet in that moment, it felt closer than ever.

This is the story of that visit.

Chapter 13

CAPT ARUN SINGH JASROTIA, AC, SM

If Chacha taught me how extraordinary courage emerged from the most ordinary homes in Haphruda, Late Captain Arun Jasrotia reminds me how even the bravest among us were never beyond the valley's reach.

Like I mentioned earlier, Kashmir valley shaped many heroes, but it also took some of the finest—the ones we could least afford to lose. Arun was one of them. A soldier whose talent, instinct, and heart could have changed the Army's future, yet whose life was cut short by the very terrain we fought to reclaim.

Heroes may rise from civilians and soldiers alike, but in the dark folds of Lolab valley not all of them get to live long enough to see what they had helped build.

You shouldn't have died, Arun! You shouldn't have.... You were too precious!

If you were alive today, you would have been a fine Brigadier or Major General on your way to becoming one of the finest Generals the Indian Army has ever seen. In your glorious professional journey, you would have inspired so many ordinary mortals, just as you had inspired me way back in the Echo Squadron in NDA.

There are some people one can't help falling in love with. He was just that person. Simple, soft-spoken, amicable, and so adorable. He was the epitome of an 'Officer and a Gentleman' that NDA inspired us to become. He was the reason for me to join

9 Para. I was so excited to meet him when I received my probation call. In fact, I had booked a telephone call for him at the Valley on the very first day of my arrival in the unit, only to find that all officers of the team were out on an operation. That night, he was operating in Balkul Gali in Lolab, which I remember was his favourite hunting ground.

The intelligence was solid. The militant group was using Balkul Gali as a temporary hideout. The night was pitch-dark, the sky smothered with clouds, rain lashing the ground in relentless sheets. It was the kind of weather that emptied roads, sealed doors, and drove ordinary men deeper into the comfort of their homes.

For a commando, this was commando weather. This was when the world slowed down, vigilance dulled, and only the toughest and most determined were willing to move. Arun knew nights like these were gifts, not obstacles. He was not going to let this one slip. If Balkul Gali had to be reached, this was the night to do it.

In our units, there is an unspoken phrase – a “lucky officer”. No one ever defines it, yet everyone knows what it means. An officer who reads the ground better than others, who sensed danger before it announced itself, whose presence tilted the odds ever so slightly in our favour. Arun Jasrotia was spoken of in those terms. “Jasrotia Sahab doesn’t talk much,” his boys would say quietly. “His rifle talks instead.”

That was the man I had come looking for.

Fate, however, had other plans. On the very night I reported to the unit, Arun was grievously wounded, hit during the same operation at Balkul Gali. I tried calling him. He was out for an operation, the radio operator had informed me. The call never went through. He was shot the same night at Balkul Gali. It still feels strange how a simple unanswered call can leave such a hollowness behind. He fought for nine days in Srinagar’s Base Hospital before finally slipping away. Though I could never meet him, every gunshot that had found him seemed to pass through me as well. It felt like losing one of my own. He was not a stranger, but a man I had followed here, only to arrive too late.

What soothed the ache, even if only briefly, were the stories his men told after he was gone. You could hear those fragments of courage, instinct, and quiet leadership that were stitched together in mess halls and corridors. Once, long after Arun had fallen, a commando looked at me and said, almost hesitantly, "Sahab, you look exactly like Jasrotia Sahab. Same face… same moustache… even the mannerisms."

It was the compliment of my life! One I would have given anything to hear from Arun himself.

Capt Arun Jasrotia was one of the first losses I suffered in 9 Para. The helplessness of losing him is still so palpable. It pains me to even imagine being in his parent's shoes. Customarily, the family of 9 Para kept visiting Arun's home at Sujanpur.

Once, while returning from a military exercise in Bilaspur in 2001, I was passing through Sujanpur along with Capt Bhati and decided to pay a visit to Arun's parents.

The day was 16th August, and incidentally, it was Arun's birthday. His parents had gone to the nearby school to feed the school children, a ritual they followed every year on his birthday. We waited as we chatted with Arun's brother and sister-in-law about him, and how he was fondly called 'Happy' at home.

I was standing in the verandah when Arun's mother opened the gate on her way in. The moment she saw me in my uniform, she started calling out hysterically— "Happy! Happy! Happy is here!" She thought her dear son had returned.

I was overwhelmed, and I did not know what to do. *Should I allow aunty the momentary joy she was feeling on seeing me, as if Arun was indeed back? Or should I break her dying heart one more time?*

I was shivering when I spoke with her. "I am sorry, aunty. I am Deep Bhagat. I was passing by and thought I should meet you." I had a lump in my throat, and I felt terribly sorry for her. The pain of watching her in that state was excruciating. I just held her quietly as she cried, remembering her son. It was brutal, if nothing more, to go through what this elderly lady was going through.

That day changed the way I looked at loss. Somewhere between unanswered calls, hospital corridors, and whispered updates, one conviction settled in quietly, I no longer wanted death to be the measure of courage. I had seen enough of it. I didn't want our sacrifices to be remembered as our *balidan*. If anything, the balidan should belong to the enemy, paid for his choices, not ours.

I wasn't naïve. Combat would always carry risk. Men would still take bullets. But experience had already taught me that many deaths weren't inevitable. They were preventable. And that responsibility did not rest with the young soldier at the front; it rested squarely with those of us who planned, equipped, trained, and sent them forward.

From that point on, leadership meant something very specific to me. It meant better weapons, sharper intelligence, and planning that bordered on obsession. It meant training hard, but training honestly, preparing men not just to fight, but to survive. Because no operation, no accolade, no badge was worth a life that was lost carelessly.

I had also begun to see how casually we spoke of dying young, as if it were the highest form of contribution. It isn't. Dying is easy. Living well, fighting smart, returning with your men – that demands far more discipline, sweat, and restraint. A living officer continues to serve the nation again and again; his death leaves behind a silence which is filled with grief.

So I made a promise to myself. I would question everything. I would never hide behind borrowed lines or blind obedience. We were not raised to *do and die*. We were raised to live, fight, and win.

We simply cannot afford to lose another Arun Jasrotia.

Dear Arun,

You will continue to live in our hearts.

It's been 30 years, and you are being missed terribly...

As I drove away that day, with Arun's mother's voice still echoing in my ears, I understood something deeper than grief. The Valley does not pause for our pain. Heroes like Arun become our compass, reminding us why we must fight smarter, protect our men better, and value every life under our command.

His memory travelled with me long after I left his home, and when duty eventually called me back to Kashmir, it was with a renewed resolve, to honour him not through words, but through every decision that would keep my soldiers alive in the unforgiving battlegrounds that he once dominated.

Chapter 14

OPERATION BEHKIPURA

The Army had begun asking for more of its airborne units. What was once designed to drop, seize ground, and hold was now expected to think deeper, strike smarter, and operate longer—often alone and far from support. This wasn't a change of badge or designation. It was a change of mindset. A different way of fighting. A different way of living.

The 4 Para was one such battalion which was standing at that crossroads. The men were tough, disciplined, and proud of their airborne legacy—but what lay ahead demanded something more. New skills had to be learned, old habits unlearned, and a culture of precision and patience had to replace sheer audacity. None of this could be taught in classrooms alone. It had to be lived.

I was asked to be part of that transition. To help take the battalion forward—to show, not explain, what the new standards looked like. There was no easing into it. Soon after I joined, the unit packed and moved into the Kashmir Valley. The idea was simple and uncompromising: the fastest way to learn Special Forces soldiering was to be tested by it.

The valley became their baptism. Operations replaced exercises. Mistakes carried consequences. Slowly, almost imperceptibly, a different unit began to emerge. Watching that transformation unfold—from airborne soldiers to thinking commandos—was an immense responsibility. It was also deeply rewarding.

Without realizing it at the time, we were writing a small piece of history—one operation at a time.

It's been ten years since Arun died. I was commanding a team of 4 Para in Rafiabad. The valley had changed in small ways, but its challenges had not. Intelligence still came wrapped in caution; villages still breathed suspicion; and every operation demanded the kind of clarity and discipline that men like Arun had lived by.

It was with this mindset, shaped by memory and responsibility, that Operation Behkipura unfolded before me.

* * *

Sector Headquarters, Handwara

Brigadier Pradhan exuded unwavering confidence in the fading glow of the setting sun, "Deep, the information is confirmed. You may like to hurry up as the operational area is part of the neighbouring sector, and you will need to tie up with their Sector Headquarters, and the local unit located closer to Behkipura." Brig Pradhan was the Sector Commander at one of the most active places in North Kashmir. My team was located in his sector. We were fellow paratroopers, and he was excited to get hold of such information and pass it on to us.

A mix of determination and certainty illuminated his face. I stood with him, the anticipation palpable in the air. Adjacent to us, his informant lingered in the shadows, a figure shrouded in secrecy. This pivotal moment was born from the confirmed intelligence centred on a little-known village named Behkipura. Militants were planning a clandestine meeting within the heart of Behkipura, an area known as Rafiabad, that was located midway between Baramulla and Handwara. My mind raced to the village of Behkipura, which was around five kilometres from our present location. It was famous for all the wrong reasons.

In military lexicon, Behkipura was known as a "black village"—a place marked by defiance, hostility, and danger. Here, the villagers weren't just bystanders; they were part of the militant machinery, their lips sealed tight against revealing any secrets to the Army. Whether out of loyalty, fear, or coercion, they were an invisible wall that protected the militants.

The intelligence Brigadier Pradhan had shared with me was a rare and precious gem, but it also came with a heavy dose of suspicion. The very accuracy of the information made it dangerous. It was almost too good to be true. What if this was a trap? In all my years in combat, I had learned to trust my instincts, and now, those instincts were whispering caution. A wise man had once told me: “If the attack seems too easy, beware! It might lead you straight into an ambush.”

That piece of advice had stuck with me, and for good reason. Militants had a reputation for playing a long game—using planted informers to pass along information so precise, so tempting, that it was almost impossible to ignore. The catch? That same informer would lead us straight into an ambush—a perfectly laid killing ground where escape would be next to impossible.

We couldn’t afford to walk into a trap. Getting ambushed was a tactical failure and meant certain death for our men. The only way to avoid it was to be unpredictable—changing our routes, our timings, and everything about our approach to the operational area. Surviving these operations was about staying one step ahead of the enemy’s mind games.

The challenge was clear: If we wanted to win this, we couldn’t just fight hard. We had to think smarter, stay unpredictable, and always expect the unexpected.

* * *

Time was slipping away, and the race against nightfall was on. Every passing minute brought us closer to the right kind of darkness. We were already deep into the latter part of the day, and soon the sun would set, ushering in a window of opportunity. The early hours of the night, free from moonlight, were our greatest ally.

'Darkness is a Commando's best friend'—we knew this truth better than most. Moving under the cover of night gave us the element of surprise. The absence of light meant invisibility, and invisibility meant survival. But we also knew the flip side of the coin: 'Light is death.' Any movement under moonlight would expose us like prey in an open field, drastically increasing the chances of detection. We had to reach our target before the moon rose.

In operations like these, the moon became as critical as ammunition. The phases of the moon shaped our plans, dictating when and how we moved, when we struck, and when we lay low. Currently, we were in the third quarter of the moon's waning phase, which meant the moon wouldn't rise until midnight.

This window of pure darkness wouldn't last long, and if we missed it, our chances of success would shrink dramatically. There would be no second chances. When it came to night, timing was everything.

Moonlight was still four hours away, and we needed to move fast. Every second mattered. We had to prepare swiftly, but tread with utmost caution. Time wasn't on our side, and in this hastily planned operation, some procedures had to be bypassed. In situations like these, you cut what you must, but you never compromise on safety or readiness.

I was still at the Sector Headquarters at Handwara. After speaking with the informer and Brig Pradhan, I picked up the secure military telephone line and called the Senior JCO at our team base, roughly two kilometres away. This was what we call a "Warning Order". In military parlance, a warning order conveys the type and duration of the operation, the number of troops required, the weapons and equipment needed, and any special instructions.

It's a no-frills, bullet-pointed message that is designed to get things rolling immediately.

I kept it crisp: "Get one troop ready under Capt Rawat for a 24-hour operation. The second troop under Capt Khadka will stay on standby. Carry personal weapons and grenades, including flash and smoke grenades. Bring two rocket launchers as well."

At this point, my mind was racing, running through the various scenarios which we could encounter. I pictured the house clearance operation, planning for every possible complication. What if we faced barricaded rooms? What if militants used villagers as human shields? I was already imagining solutions, mentally ticking off the gear we'd need for each challenge. The gears in my mind turned at full throttle—no room for error.

When I arrived at the team base, 24 soldiers stood ready, primed for action under Capt Rawat's command. There was no hesitation in their eyes, just silent focus. These men knew the stakes, and they trusted me to lead them through it. Capt Rawat was as reliable as they come – a warrior who never let pressure crack his calm exterior. But I knew that beneath that calm lay a mind that was constantly at work, thinking three steps ahead.

Rawat and I had worked side by side since I took over as Bravo team leader. He was sharp, honest, and unflinching; a man who called things exactly as he saw them. I had learned to appreciate that quality in him. Having people like him in the team kept us grounded and made our planning foolproof.

The men were ready. The plan was forming. We had only one shot at this, and we weren't going to miss it.

I gathered the entire team and laid out the situation in detail. These men weren't just fighters, they were seasoned professionals with sharp tactical minds. Their input was always invaluable. I trusted them to follow orders, as also to analyze with clarity and realism the information that we had received.

We discussed the intel from the informer, the impending meeting of key militant leaders. From the details provided, it was clear that this was no ordinary gathering of the militants. Leaders from different militant factions were expected to attend, which meant the stakes were high. Precautions would be extreme, and we had to assume that these militants would pull every trick in the book to protect themselves.

My men's experience showed through as we broke down the likely tactics the militants would use. We had seen these patterns before; militants didn't just stroll into villages. Their movements were deliberate, shrouded in secrecy, and known only to a select few. They moved like shadows, and only those who absolutely needed to know their plans would be briefed. Routes and timings were never fixed, they were changed at the last possible moment to avoid detection.

Even the meeting spot inside the village wouldn't be finalized until the last minute, and that location could change without warning. We knew better than to expect all the militants to gather in a single house. The leaders would be well-guarded, with lookouts positioned in nearby houses to scan for any signs of an Army patrol. In the event of a confrontation with us, the leaders would escape without hesitation, leaving others behind to fight or sacrifice themselves. Loyalty and sacrifice were currency among these groups, and promotions came to those who proved their worth in clashes with security forces.

Over time, I had developed a reluctant respect for the militants. They were masters of evasion, with an uncanny sixth sense that warned them of danger before it even appeared. Their ability to disappear at the slightest hint of a trap was almost supernatural. More often than not, they slipped through our fingers.

What made them so effective was their intelligence network. The villagers were their eyes and ears, reporting our movements and keeping the militants one step ahead. In these villages, we weren't just up against a handful of fighters; we were contending with an entire web of informants. The whole community was complicit, willingly or otherwise.

We knew that catching them at their intended meeting site would require more than just skill. It would require luck, and luck wasn't something we could count on. If we wanted to succeed, we had to outthink them, anticipate their every move, and stay ahead of their game.

This wasn't going to be easy, but then again, it never was.

* * *

I could feel butterflies churning in my stomach, and my mind refused to rest, ticking like a clock on overdrive. As we prepared to move out, every possible contingency played out one after another in my head. The disadvantages weighed heavily on us, and the more I thought about them, the clearer it became – *the odds were not in our favour.*

We were walking into unknown territory. None of us had ever been to Behkipura before. Our knowledge of the terrain was poor, and we didn't know the layout of the village—its narrow lanes, by-lanes, and alleyways were a mystery to us. We had not seen the target house, not even in a photograph. We did not know its location and the area around the house. And to make matters worse, we didn't know the villagers or their habits. All we knew was that they weren't friendly. They had no reason to help us, and we couldn't expect any favours.

On the other hand, the militants had the upper hand in every way. They knew the village intimately, having visited it many times. They could navigate the streets and alleys blindfolded if they needed to. The villagers were on their side. Whether through loyalty, fear, or manipulation, the militants had their support.

The element of initiative was with them. They had the power to call off the meeting at any moment if they sensed anything unusual. All it would take was one suspicious movement—one shadow out of place—and the whole operation would crumble. And then there was the nagging doubt about the information we'd been given. It felt almost too good to be true. Was this just another wild goose chase?

The uncertainty gnawed at me. There were too many unknowns, and that always made me uneasy. But we had to move forward. At best, I could draft a plan now, but knowing fully well that we'd need to adjust everything on the fly once we reached the village. Nothing could be finalized until we were on the ground.

As the minutes ticked by, the tension didn't ease. I felt that familiar knot of anxiety tightening in my chest. It was the kind of anxiety that comes when you know things could spiral out of control in the blink of an eye. And yet, I had to stay composed. Anxiety couldn't cloud my judgment. Patience was key. We would move in carefully, adapt as we went, and take things one step at a time.

Plans could change. Situations could unravel. But we would be ready—no matter what awaited us in Behkipura.

The Plan

The objective was clear: create a loose cordon around the main house and the peripheral houses. We knew the militants wouldn't gather in one place; they were too cautious about that. They would be spread across multiple houses, with lookouts stationed in different locations to monitor for any signs of an Army patrol. If we focused only on the core house, we'd leave too many gaps for them to exploit. That's why the cordon had to extend to the surrounding houses, to cut off any escape routes and to contain the entire area.

Our search plan was simple, but deliberate. We wouldn't rush in blindly at night. Instead, we'd maintain tight surveillance throughout the night, watching for any movement or signs of activity. At daybreak, we would begin clearing the houses one by one, working from the outermost houses towards the centre, ensuring nothing was missed. This method would help in flushing out any lookouts or militants hiding in the periphery and prevent them from slipping through unnoticed. Every movement had to be controlled, precise, and silent

Vigilance would be key. Every house in the cordon had to remain under constant surveillance throughout the night. The slightest sound or shadow could be a sign of movement, and we had to be ready to react. But for this to work, we needed complete silence and total darkness.

* * *

After briefing the troops at Langaiyat, we rolled out. The vehicles carried us only so far—to a point beyond the hearing range of Behkipura. There, we left the vehicles behind and continued the rest of the journey on foot.

It was a dark night, with no moonlight to betray our presence. The world around us felt heavy with silence, as if the entire valley was holding its breath. We moved quietly, every step measured, weaving through the narrow lanes and by-lanes of the village. The tension was thick in the air, but the silence worked in our favour.

And then, something strange hit me. As we slipped deeper into the village, I realized there were no dogs. This was unusual, and it didn't sit right. In villages like these, dogs were the first line of defence. They barked at strangers, at movement, at anything out of the ordinary. Their absence was unnatural.

Then it dawned on me – this had to be part of the militants' strategy. No dogs, no barking, no alarms. It was a clever tactic, designed to conceal their movements when they visited the village. Without barking dogs, they could come and go as they pleased, slipping undetected through the shadows.

But tonight, that same strategy worked in our favour. The absence of dogs meant that we could move without triggering any alarms. The eerie silence that had first unsettled me was now our ally. We moved like ghosts, closing in undetected on the target house, our presence a secret the night kept safe.

Even though everything seemed to be going according to plan, my instincts refused to let me relax. Something didn't sit right. My mind kept circling back to the informant. He was an unknown element, a wildcard, and in our line of work, those can get you killed. Normally, we run thorough checks before trusting anyone with operational intel. Building trust with an informant isn't just about one conversation or a handshake. It takes time, consistency, and observation. But this instance, time wasn't on our side.

We had no choice but to go with Brigadier Pradhan's word. He vouched for the man, and that had to be enough. Yet, combat experience had ingrained one golden rule in me: 'Respect all, but suspect all.' No matter how valuable the information, my mind kept whispering warnings. What if this guy wasn't as reliable as he seemed? What if he was leading us into an ambush? In operations like this, especially when they're thrown together at the last minute, danger lurks around every corner. Trusting too soon could cost lives.

During the planning phase, I put him to the test. I asked him which route we should take to the target house. He answered confidently, laying out a path he claimed was the best. But I deliberately overruled him, choosing a route that was longer, more difficult, and far less predictable. It wasn't the easy way, but in situations like these, easy is often deadly. I wasn't about to let speed and convenience compromise safety.

To stay one step ahead, I assigned one of my sharpest men to stick with the informant, shadowing him at every turn. His job was simple – watch him like a hawk. The buddy system was a lifeline. I wanted eyes on this man, assessing his every movement, every gesture. A single twitch, hesitation, anything out of place would be a warning bell. When you're walking into the lion's den, you can't afford to miss even the smallest detail.

The operation was moving forward, but in the back of my mind, a voice whispered: What if we're walking into a trap?

We reached the target house just past midnight. The silence around it was dense, almost oppressive, the kind that sharpened every sense. Darkness still held, but not for long—the moon was threatening to break through at any moment. Time was no longer on our side. We needed to deploy immediately.

As planned, we split into squads of five men, each team moving like shadows through the darkness. Everyone knew their role. With precision and stealth, we spread out, loosely cordoning the entire area and settling into our ambush and surveillance positions.

One by one, I quietly went to each squad, confirming their tasks. Everyone understood the stakes. This was the kind of mission where the smallest mistake could get someone killed. Our men were sharp, but we were operating under a heavy fog of tension. One wrong move, one miscommunication, and we could end up firing at our own people. This was a real possibility, something I had witnessed before in the chaos of night operations. Blue-on-blue casualties—friendly fire—was always a lurking danger.

To prevent any mishap, I made sure everyone knew the general positions of the other squads. Once we settled into our locations, no one was to move. No exceptions. Even the slightest shift without warning could trigger a firefight between our own parties. The silence we maintained was our lifeline, and the success of the mission depended on it. At the same time, I reminded every man that our primary focus was the target house. It had to remain under constant, undivided surveillance.

* * *

The night dragged on, the cold biting through our jackets and creeping into our bones. The month of March in the valley is unforgiving. We were shivering, muscles aching from the cold and the tension. It was the kind of cold that settles in your joints and stays there, wearing you down slowly. But no one complained. The thought of what might happen at first light kept us going. Tomorrow would bring the action we had prepared for, or the unexpected twist we hadn't seen coming.

Radio silence remained in place. No chatter, no unnecessary transmissions. Every man sat quietly in his position, waiting for what was to come. The quiet was suffocating, as if the night itself was holding its breath. And though everything seemed to be unfolding as planned, I knew better than to get comfortable.

Around 3 am, the night stirred. Muffled voices cut through the silence. Torches flickered to life inside the target house, thin blades of light slashed through the darkness. Shouts followed—hurried, urgent. Something was unfolding.

Either someone had arrived… or someone was about to leave.

We couldn't see enough to be certain. The shadows refused to give anything away. But opportunity rarely announces itself clearly in the dark. This might be our only window. One signal, and we could storm into the house and end it—*if* the militants were inside.

Civilians moving at this hour, in the dead of winter, was unlikely. Not impossible—but unlikely.

I weighed the seconds. Act now and risk a mistake, or hesitate and let them slip away forever.

The temptation to act was strong. I could feel the tension building in my squad, as if everyone was waiting for me to give the green light to storm into the house. The idea clawed at me – hit them now, under cover of night, and catch them off guard. But experience whispered caution. I'd learned the hard way that impulsive actions in operations like these only create chaos. This wasn't some training exercise. A midnight raid without coordination was asking for disaster.

Using radios to alert my other teams was also out of the question. Militants constantly monitor frequencies, and the smallest transmission could betray our position and intent. If the enemy caught wind of us, they'd vanish into the night like smoke. Worse, in the pitch-black confusion, our squads could easily mistake each other for the enemy and open fire. That would be a nightmare.

Even more troubling was the possibility of collateral damage. If civilians got caught in the crossfire, it would not only jeopardize our mission but also turn the entire village against us. That was a cost I was not willing to pay, no matter what. The escape of a few militants would be far more acceptable than the blood of innocents on our hands.

I took a deep breath, forcing myself to think clearly. Charging in now would mean abandoning everything that we had planned. We had to stick to the strategy, even if it gnawed at me. We would wait. Dawn was only a few hours away. Morning light would give us the clarity to act decisively and without mistakes.

This night wasn't over yet, and neither was our mission.

* * *

As the first light of day cracked the horizon, the air seemed to shift. The night's oppressive stillness gave way to a world bathed in the cold morning light. At precisely 0500 Hours, I gave the nod, and my Senior JCO, Subedar Ram, and I rushed towards the target house. Everything looked different in daylight. The eerie quiet was gone, and the village now felt almost normal. But that sense of normalcy only made me more uneasy.

The house we approached was a three-storey structure made of stone and wood, looming over the surrounding area. It was old and weathered, with numerous rooms, each with a window that faced outwards. The façade alone had at least 36 windows, any one of which could conceal a threat. Those windows were watching us, and standing under them made the hairs on the back of my neck prickle.

Sub Ram knocked on the door, and I stood to the side, my weapon trained on the entrance. The sound of heavy footsteps echoed from inside. My grip tightened on my rifle, anticipating some action.

Then, without warning, the door burst open, and chaos spilled into the street. A civilian man shot out of the house, head down, muttering something incomprehensible as he sprinted away. I tried to stop him, my voice firm, but he dodged past me like a rabbit fleeing a snare. Before I could process what had happened, a woman carrying a baby in her arms rushed out right behind him, her face twisted with panic. She didn't even look at us as she bolted. It was as if we didn't exist.

I was about to signal Sub Ram when another man appeared in the doorway, pushing past us.

"Where do you think you're going?" I barked, blocking his path.

"To the washroom," he stammered, pointing vaguely towards the distance before darting away without waiting for a response.

And then more of them came – three more residents, slipping out of the house one after another, fear etched on their faces. They were fleeing. And suddenly, it clicked. These people weren't just escaping the house; they were running from something inside.

The realization hit me like a jolt of electricity. There had to be militants inside, and the residents knew that a firefight was inevitable. They were getting out before bullets started flying.

My pulse quickened. Sub Ram and I were standing right at the entrance, vulnerable and exposed. We were in the worst possible position: directly beneath the windows, an easy target if anyone inside decided to fire or toss a grenade. We were sitting ducks.

"We need to move. Now!" I whispered sharply to Sub Ram. He caught on immediately, his sharp instincts kicking in. We slipped out of the danger zone in a few quick strides, putting distance between us and the house. I could feel the weight of unseen eyes watching us from behind those windows. Whatever was inside, it was dangerous, and it was waiting.

Once out of harm's way, I glanced at Sub Ram. "There's something fishy, Sahab. We'll reorganize properly and then move in," I said. He gave a quick nod, understanding exactly what I meant without another word. The house was too dangerous to storm into without a better plan.

We quickly reworked our strategy. If this was the core house, we couldn't afford any surprises from the neighbouring houses. We decided to clear every single peripheral house in the vicinity before making our final move. It had to be thorough. No shortcuts. No room for error.

The next few hours crawled by as we meticulously cleared each house. Every door, every room, and every corner was checked with precision. No militants, no suspicious movements, just empty spaces and nervous villagers. By 10 am, we had completed the search of the entire area. Only one house remained.

Now, it was time to finish what we had started. We surrounded the house from all sides, our men in position. The stage was set.

The first step was crucial: we needed confirmation. Up until now, our suspicions were built solely on the strange behaviour of the house's residents that morning. But when we pressed them for answers, they all denied that any militants were inside. They swore that the house was clear, but their panicked exodus told a different story. Something didn't add up.

I knew we needed more than gut feelings and hunches. We needed solid information and I decided to try a little game of psychology.

I scanned the crowd of villagers that had gathered around, their faces a mix of fear and curiosity. I singled out a young girl and a nervous-looking man. I asked them both, separately, to go inside the house and open all the windows on every floor. It was a subtle but deliberate move. If they were hiding something, they might hesitate.

The girl was fearless. Without missing a beat, she walked confidently into the house, her footsteps echoing through the quiet. She moved swiftly to the first floor and flung open the windows. Then, leaning out, she challenged us boldly. "There's no one here. Come and see for yourself!"

Her confidence was unsettling, and for a moment, I almost believed her. She sounded too sure, too perfect. But something about the situation didn't sit right. I shifted my attention to the other man, the one who looked pale and uneasy. He shuffled nervously under my gaze, a man clearly out of his depth. He was the key.

I had used this tactic before, and it had worked like a charm. Confidence could unnerve people, especially those holding onto a secret. Instead of asking the obvious question, "Are the militants inside?", I cornered the man and, with deliberate authority, asked: "Which floor are they hiding on?"

The question was precise, intentional, and dripping with certainty. It wasn't a guess; it was a statement which was disguised as a question. It left no room for denial. From the way I asked, the man probably thought I already knew the answer. All I needed was confirmation of their location.

His defences crumbled almost immediately. He glanced around nervously, as if looking for a way out, then blurted, "Second floor."

I kept my expression neutral, hiding the thrill that shot through me. "How many?" I asked calmly, as if we were discussing the weather.

"Two."

There it was! The confirmation I had been waiting for. Two militants. Second floor. The information landed like a missing puzzle piece falling perfectly into place.

But I didn't let the man see my satisfaction. Showing excitement could spook the crowd or tip off anyone watching. I nodded, as if his answer was exactly what I expected, and sent him on his way.

With the intel locked in, I moved deliberately. No rush, no urgency, just a soldier on a routine check. I calmly walked from one teammate to the next, delivering the critical information in hushed tones – "Two militants, second floor."

The noose was tightening. Now, we knew exactly where they were, and they had no idea we were coming.

* * *

Now came the hard part, the decision. With the militants confirmed inside, I stood at crossroads. Two options lay before us, and both came with their own set of consequences. Neither choice was easy.

The first option was to storm the house. It was the bold, chivalrous route, but also the riskiest. In combat, physically clearing houses is a deadly game where the odds are stacked heavily against the attacker. Inside those walls, every step could be your last. The internal layout of Kashmiri village houses was notoriously complicated – small rooms, tight entrances, and narrow passageways that connected the rooms like a maze. Moving from one room to another was like walking into a death trap.

These entrances were what we called "fatal funnels"—narrow choke points where movement is restricted, and the enemy can anticipate where you'll be. Most casualties happen at these very points, as there's no space to manoeuvre, no cover to shield you, and no time to react if the enemy strikes. If even one of us got injured inside, the whole operation could spiral into chaos. Every second spent dragging an injured soldier out would multiply the risk for everyone else.

For the militants, this was a battle for survival. They had nothing to lose. If we stormed the house, they would fight with the desperation of cornered men, knowing this was likely their last stand. And if they could hold us off until nightfall, their odds of escape would skyrocket. Night was their ally, and they knew every inch of this terrain better than we did. The house was their fortress, and we would be the intruders.

The second option was simpler but far more destructive – razing the house to the ground. A barrage of rocket launcher fire would obliterate the building, leaving nothing but rubble. Tactically, it was safer. No need to risk lives, no need to storm dangerous rooms. We'd just flatten everything. But this option came with a cost that no amount of tactical logic could justify.

Destroying a house in front of the villagers wasn't just about eliminating a target. It sent the kind of message we did not want to send. The explosion might kill the militants, but it would also destroy the fragile trust which we had worked so hard to build with the local population. In a war for hearts and minds, the Army would lose generations of goodwill in a single blast. The sight of their home reduced to ashes would plant seeds of hatred in the hearts of their children. These children would grow up with that memory etched into their minds, and one day, they might pick up arms against us.

For me, that was the real danger. A violent action might win the day, but it would cost us the future. And no victory, no matter how tactically sound, was worth turning more people against us. I wasn't willing to walk that path.

So, there I stood, weighing these two options.

It was now 2 pm, and the situation on the ground was shifting against us. The longer we stayed, the more restless the villagers became. Their routine was disrupted, and their frustration was boiling over. Groups of locals started gathering near the house, chanting slogans against the Army, their voices growing louder by the minute.

But I knew better than to take their anger at face value. This was a distraction, plain and simple. The militants knew how to manipulate these situations, and the villagers were more than willing accomplices. If we made even the slightest mistake, if we lost focus for even a moment, the militants would slip through our cordon, hidden among the villagers. It was a dangerous game, and time was not on our side.

I needed a new plan, and fast. The clock was ticking. By 5 pm, the light would start to fade, and with nightfall, the militants would have a hundred ways of escaping. The villagers would help them blend into the darkness, and our entire operation would be for nothing.

I knew I couldn't storm the house without risking my men. A direct assault would be a bloodbath. At the same time, obliterating the house with explosives wasn't an option either.

Then, an idea sparked.

The solution was in the riot control equipment!

A few days ago, I'd spoken with a Police Inspector at Handwara. He had shown me the types of riot control equipment that were generally held by the police force. He showed me chili grenades—non-lethal weapons that were fired from a rifle's barrel with a range of 50 to 75 metres. When fired, these grenades release a cloud of chili flakes so potent that they make your eyes and nose burn instantly. The inspector had explained how effective they were at breaking up riots.

And that's when it struck me: If the chili grenade could drive crowds out of open spaces, what would it do in the confined rooms of that house?

Without wasting a second, I dispatched a JCO to the Handwara police station, instructing him to bring back as many chili grenades as he could carry. The police obliged without hesitation. But it would take the JCO an hour to return, and until then, I needed to manage the growing tension with the villagers.

The crowd was getting bolder by the minute. The chanting grew louder, and their frustration was palpable. I could see it in their eyes. They were waiting for us to make a wrong move. If we tried to push them back by force, we'd be playing right into their hands. One shove, one harsh word, and the situation would explode. The militants inside the house would seize the moment to escape in the chaos.

I had to buy time.

I scanned the crowd, searching for a way to diffuse the tension. I called the village elders away from the crowd, pulling them aside for a quiet conversation. Now, this was a game of subtlety, a battle of wits.

I kept my voice calm and measured, assuring them that we weren't certain if militants were inside the house. "We'll be wrapping up soon," I told them, carefully planting the idea that the

Army would be moving out shortly. The elders exchanged glances, the tension in their shoulders easing. They thought they had won. In their minds, the Army was about to leave, and the militants inside the house would remain safe.

It worked. The agitation cooled. The shouting subsided, and the villagers began to disperse, satisfied that the threat to their hidden allies was almost over.

Now, all I had to do was wait for the JCO to return with the chili grenades. The militants didn't know it yet, but time was running out for them.

Relief washed over me as I spotted the Maruti Gypsy rolling in, dust kicking up beneath its wheels. The JCO hopped out, carrying the chili rifle grenade equipment, and quickly handed it over to the teams. Not another second was wasted.

Since this was a new weapon for us, a quick crash course was in order. In a matter of minutes, our team members familiarized themselves with loading and firing the grenades. Every second counted, but my men were sharp, picking it up with ease. As the sun dipped lower over the horizon, we spread out, taking strategic firing positions around the house.

The windows of the house were already open, an advantage we wouldn't waste. From every side, we aimed and fired the chili grenades through the windows, each shot releasing a payload of irritating chili dust that clung to the air inside. The grenades hissed as they detonated, their payload filling the rooms with an invisible, burning cloud.

In open spaces, the gas would have dissipated in moments. But in the tight confines of the house, it lingered like a suffocating mist, turning every breath into an ordeal. The air became a torment, clawing at the militants' lungs and stinging their eyes and noses.

What had been their sanctuary only minutes ago was now an unbearable prison.

The response was almost immediate. Within two minutes, the first militant cracked. Gasping and overwhelmed, he made the desperate choice of escaping the torture. With no other way out, he threw himself from the second-floor window.

We were ready. He hit the ground hard, breaking both legs, but there was no time for mercy. In a flash, our men neutralized him before he could retaliate.

The second militant lasted only a few moments longer. Disoriented and desperate, he scrambled from one room to another, hoping to find refuge from the relentless burn. But there was nowhere left to hide. Finally, he made a break for it, stumbling down the stairs and towards the front door.

The moment he appeared at the entrance, our waiting team finished the job. Clean and swift. The threat was eliminated without a single casualty on our side.

In less than five minutes, it was all over. Two militants were neutralized. No civilians were harmed, no excessive violence; and the house stood intact – a testament to clear thinking and tactical precision.

We searched the bodies of the slain militants, gathered weapons and documents, and swiftly retreated, leaving nothing behind. The operation had been a success, not just in neutralizing the militants, but in preserving the fragile trust of the villagers. We left the scene without fanfare, silent and efficient, like shadows disappearing into the dusk.

The next day, a small column in the local newspaper read: "Encounter with militants happened in the area of Behkipura, Rafiabad: Two militants were killed in a day-long encounter. However, the troops who killed the militants remain unidentified."

I clipped the article, laminated it, and tucked it into my scrapbook. This was how it was supposed to be. No glory, no names in the headlines. Just a job done right, quietly, and effectively. This is what we stood for. This is what it means to be Special Forces.

Chapter 15
CONQUERING FEAR

July, 2012

Behkipura ended, but it didn't leave me easily. In the valley, the enemy was rarely seen. He existed in pauses, in wrong assumptions, in the way fear travelled faster than facts. I had seen how that fear shaped people, soldiers and civilians alike, and how dangerous it became when it went unrecognised.

Over time, I realized that fear was never the problem. Not in Kashmir, not in combat, not in life. The problem was what we did with it.

Somewhere after those operations, my journey brought me back to a place I loved—the Commando Wing. It was there that experiences from the field found meaning. Teaching young soldiers allowed me to pass on what the valley had taught me, even as I continued to learn myself. Every incident, every mistake, every adventure added another layer of understanding.

One of those lessons came in an unexpected form. It involved fear, control, and a snake.

Commando Wing, Belgaum

The Military Secretary (MS) branch of the Army HQ may issue postings for the entire Army, but they say that the MS branch doesn't do postings for the Commando Wing. God does the posting. This is arguably the pinnacle of postings in the Indian Army, where some of the fittest, happiest, and most spirited officers serve as Commando instructors.

Securing an instructor grade at the Commando Course is no small feat. Over a span of 32 gruelling days, the commandos face an astonishing array of 36 tests, each designed to push them to their limits. These tests aren't for the faint-hearted and weak-kneed. They include speed marches of 5 km, 10 km, 20 km, 30 km, and even 40 km, alongside a rigorous suite of challenges such as mountaineering, navigating treacherous terrains both by day and by night, and conquering a demanding battle obstacle course. And just when you think you've reached your physical limit, the Commando ethos kicks in – mental agility is just as crucial. Commandos face written examinations on explosives, tactics, and more, often juggling multiple tests in a single day. Maintaining peak physical condition throughout this intense regimen is no easy task, but the foundations laid during training at NDA make it possible.

Interestingly, many commandos hesitate to return as instructors, daunted by the sheer volume of the physical demands. Yet, those who excel in the course and return to Belgaum soon discover the extraordinary camaraderie of this elite posting. Here, fit, tough, hardworking go-getters form a remarkable team. Time flows differently in the Commando Wing; it rushes forward and is fuelled by adrenaline and determination.

Life at the Commando School is unparalleled – action-packed, relentless, and exhilarating. Every hour of the day is a whirlwind of activity; there's no pause, no slow moments. Even during course breaks, the energy never wanes. Officers engage in a unique version of golf, sprinting between holes while toting their clubs on their backs, a testament to their unyielding spirit and zest for life

There is always something happening. Instructors would either be running, playing, scaling rock faces, handling explosives, or slithering down artificial platforms. But the real fun was at the snake pit. Amid the rigorous climbing and commando drills, all of us would take time to handle the serpents. The Commando Wing officers had become Belgaum's unofficial snake handlers, always ready to spring into action whenever a snake was spotted anywhere in the neighbourhood. These snakes weren't treated as threats; they were kept as pets within the Commando Wing, a testament to our unique skills and courage.

Our snake collection was diverse – agile rat snakes, revered and deadly cobras with a commanding presence, and silent yet lethal vipers and kraits. Every instructor at Commando Wing would be trained in snake handling, starting with the non-venomous rat snakes. As confidence grew, they progressed to handling cobras, and only the most skilled dared to work with vipers and kraits.

Like every other commando instructor, I was drawn to this test of fear. However, like almost everyone in the country, I'd grown up with an instinctual aversion to snakes. They seemed slimy, dangerous, and unpredictable. Yet here, at Commando Wing, snake handling was taught as a test of courage and a method to conquer our deepest fears. The snakes represented the deep fears in our hearts. We were being trained to boldly stand in front of our fears and face them, yet not be foolhardy at the same time.

I wasn't immune to that fear. Snakes always unsettled me. And today was no different. I stood before Major Johny Malik, my instructor and mentor in snake handling. Johny had a natural ease with these creatures; the snakes seemed to trust him, moving calmly in his presence. His demonstrations were flawless, making snake handling look effortless. Despite being younger than me in rank and age, Johny exuded wisdom and confidence that earned him our unwavering respect. Strong yet humble, skilled yet always eager to learn, Johny was the epitome of what a commando should be.

Johny led me into the snake pit. It was a circular enclosure where the snakes moved freely. Today, a single rat snake coiled gracefully in the center, its eyes fixed on us. The air was thick with tension as I took a deep breath, trying to steady my nerves.

Johny began the briefing with his usual directness. "Sir, today you'll handle the rat snake. It's non-venomous, so there's no danger even if it bites you." His voice was calm and authoritative. "Just remember, it's quick. If you don't handle it properly, it'll wriggle out of your hands."

"Sure, buddy," I replied, forcing a confident tone despite the knot of anxiety in my stomach.

I realized that courage needs to be nurtured, and the best way to gain courage is to act.

"Let me see what happens next," I thought as I stepped into the snake pit.

This five-foot-long snake was slowly crawling away from me. I am sure half his eyes were towards me as he waited for any movement from my side.

I made my move. I went after its tail and grabbed it firmly as I picked up the snake. As if it knew what would happen, it reacted instantly, thrashing in my grip, jerking its body towards me. Instinctively, I pulled my hand back, still holding on to the snake. Only my grip tightened and I held him more firmly.

The snake was in pain, but I cared little. My brain was being bombarded by the hormones that are secreted by fear. Instinctively, my grip got tighter. I was only thinking about myself. The snake made more jerky actions. It could not reach my hand, but it could reach the bottom of my jeans. It bit my jeans, and its teeth broke in the process.

I was now in a panic. In an instant, I threw the snake away from me. It hit the floor with a thud. I had inadvertently hurt the snake. As it lay there, probably in pain, I climbed back from the snake pit. Maj Johny was quietly watching all this from the edge.

Then he spoke. "Sir, do you know why you reacted in this manner?"

I was quiet, recovering from the trauma that I had just undergone. Maj Johny continued, "Because you were afraid of this snake. There was fear in your heart. That's the reason you reacted so violently." He paused, letting the words sink in.

"I want you to try another approach, sir."

I watched Johny as he was about to teach me one of the most profound lessons of my life: "Treat this snake like a child. Handle it softly. Make sure that the snake is comfortable in your hands. Make it feel comfortable as you would make any kid comfortable. You need to fall in love with this creature."

I listened to him and absorbed what he had just said. My entire body relaxed immediately. Every word that Johny said resonated with my inner being. Suddenly, there was no fear. It had just dissipated. In its place, only warmth, compassion, and love took root. I entered the snake pit again, kneeling beside the snake. It was lying coiled, probably reeling from the pain that I had induced. My heart pounded, yet I was surprisingly calm. I touched the snake calmly and softly, and I waited. It lay there without making any movement. Then, I started caressing its body. It was relaxed, too, as I picked it up. I was still nervous from within. What if the snake strikes me now? It's so much closer to my face. I watched it intently and calmly. I quietly spoke to myself: "Have faith in the power of love. Everything will be fine."

Feeling relaxed, the snake turned and climbed up my hand, then turned and moved slowly over my arm. I was trembling from within, yet I maintained a calm demeanour. My faith in Maj Johny's words was being put to test. The snake was okay, and I was okay.

It was a moment of quiet triumph over my fear, over the snake, and myself. Meanwhile, Maj Johny took a couple of pictures as I finished my first lesson on snake handling. I had not only learned to handle snakes but also to handle people, situations, and my fears.

Through this experience, I uncovered a powerful truth. Much of what drives us as individuals and communities is rooted in fear. As I reflected on it further, the way people behave and react to others began to make perfect sense. We are often governed not by logic or understanding, but by the fears we carry within us… fears that have accumulated over time, shaped by stories, prejudices, and propaganda. These fears cloud our minds, thus forcing us into defensive postures and making us react with aggression towards anything or anyone unfamiliar.

How often do we instinctively mistrust someone from a different community, culture, or background? It's rarely because of personal experience, but more because of the narratives we've been fed over time. These stories become the lens through which we see the world, making us believe that others pose a threat, even when they don't. Whether it's distrust towards people of different faiths, nations, or even colleagues at work, our first reaction often comes from a place of fear, not understanding.

This realization hit me hard. I knew I had to change the way I navigated my professional and personal life. And surprisingly, I didn't have to force this change; it came naturally. The first step was to become aware of the fears being planted in me. Whenever I felt hostility or mistrust creeping in, I paused and asked myself: *Where is this fear coming from? Is it based on real experience or someone else's narrative?* I began to question the fears that others tried to instill in me. I questioned my own instincts.

This shift changed everything. I realized that if I didn't let fear dictate my actions, I could see people and situations more clearly. I became more empathetic, more understanding, and less reactive. Instead of reacting with anger or suspicion, I found myself approaching situations with curiosity and patience.

In high-pressure military situations, fear can take hold of even the most seasoned soldiers. Fuelled by fear, our reactions become more violent and disproportionate than the situation demands. In such moments, we unwittingly play into the hands of those who understand human psychology better than we do, i.e. our enemies. They know how fear warps judgment, and they exploit it, knowing that reckless actions only deepen the divide and create more instability.

* * *

Later, in places like Kashmir, I would recognize that same tension again, the kind that tightens your body before you even know why. The enemy was different, the stakes far higher, but the feeling was familiar. Fear didn't announce itself loudly. It crept in quietly, disguised as urgency, suspicion, and the need to act first.

The snake had taught me something simple. Force was rarely the answer. Panic made things worse. Stillness, awareness, and restraint mattered more than speed or aggression.

I carried that lesson with me. Not as a rule, not as a theory—but as a habit. Whether it was a snake, a situation, or a man standing across from me, I learned to pause, read, and understand before reacting.

Fear never disappeared.

But it stopped controlling my hands.

Chapter 16

SKYDIVING: TRAUMA AND TRIUMPH

January, 2015
Skydiving: My Dream

Skydiving had always been a dream I clung to—a dream that wouldn't let go of me. It took root back in 1995 when I was still on probation. Maj, now Lt Gen Paramjit Sangha (Retd) had brought me along in a helicopter to coordinate skydiving jumps. I was seated in the same chopper as Maj Paramjit in the front seat while three skydivers were sitting in the rear seat of this small helicopter. I was merely a coordinator between the jumpers and the Drop Zone. But what I witnessed changed everything. When Maj Paramjit dived out of that helicopter, plunging into the void with the ease of a bird on a breeze, I was filled with awe. A fire was ignited.

A dream was born, something that would not let me sleep. That image haunted my nights. I could see him spiralling down, fearless and graceful. I knew that, someday, that would be me. As a Special Forces officer, we were required to specialize in either Combat Deep Sea Diving or Combat Sky Diving as part of our professional qualifications. When given the choice between becoming a deep-sea diver or a skydiver, the answer was instant. I didn't want to swim in the water. I wanted to swim in the sky.

But dreams have their way of testing you. The Army was running short on parachutes, and skydiving opportunities were sparse. Later, I volunteered for Combat Free Fall training, but life threw another obstacle my way. A cardiac problem was diagnosed during the stringent Air Force medicals, and my name was pulled back from the Free Fall course. Twenty long years passed, and my dream was left hanging in the air, waiting.

Finally, at the age of 47, my chance came. I discovered that Skydiving courses are conducted throughout the world. I researched and chose Skydiving Dubai as my preferred place of learning.

Skydiving, at my age, seemed reckless to most. Why would I take on such an adrenaline-pumping high-speed sport at the dusk of my life, when I was nearing fifty?

The answer to this question was something more profound. There was a candid desire to conquer my proverbial Everest! I wanted to check if I still had the energy, courage, and belief in myself that had made me a Special Forces officer two decades ago. It was about proving to myself that the fire inside me hadn't dimmed.

I had jumped out of an airplane before. I must have done 20-odd static line jumps in the last two decades from heights no more than 1,500 feet.

Skydiving was different and more adventurous. Skydivers jump from heights of more than 10,000 feet without opening their parachutes. These are opened only after one reaches a height of 4,000 feet or less. Till then, one falls freely in the open sky. Skydivers have always fascinated me; their ease in the air, their seeming invincibility. They are achievers in their own way. I wanted to be one of them. Not just falling but flying, owning the skies like they did. How majestic!

While watching a training movie on skydiving skills created by the US Army, one particular action caught my attention. It was a jump out from an aircraft by a demonstrating student. It was the vault of confidence in himself and god. The spring action of that leap stunned me into inertia. My mind got glued to that very poise.

I asked myself – Would I have the same spring as I jump out, or would I go out with a heavy heart pulling me back?

My son Akshaj, only 15 at that time, who was watching the same movie, asked me a more fundamental question. "Dad, will you be able to jump out?" I looked at him pensively and confidently assured him that I was sure I would.

His words echoed in my mind. *Could I? What if I failed?* But the dream was too strong. I had to know if I still dared to conquer my fears.

* * *

Before heading to Dubai, I was consumed by thoughts that battled against my decision.

Logically, my desire to do skydiving jumps at this age and stage did not fit into any scheme. Starting a new venture like skydiving at such a late stage of life would lead me nowhere. I had responsibilities. Any accident or mishap would land the entire family in a soup. This was the time my kids required me the most. My adventure should not cost them dearly. Was this worth risking it all?

Such an adventure would have been understandable had it been carried out some 20–25 years ago, when I was younger and a bachelor, when I was not carrying the responsibility of a full-fledged family. Tragically, such training was not available then. All this has mushroomed in the previous few years.

My father has been my biggest cheerleader throughout my life. He has never opposed any of my professional or personal decisions except for two. The first was when I volunteered for the Special Forces Battalion, and the second was now. After a lot of contemplating and a long silence, he finally asked me, "Why are you doing this, son?"

"This is my bucket list, Dad. This is one of the things I want to do before I die." I told him.

Despite the crests and troughs of apprehension and determination clouding my mind and heart, I still decided to go ahead and learn skydiving in Dubai. It was a monumental decision. The only plausible reason was that I profoundly desired to skydive, to experience the freefall. I wanted to fly majestically in the air, narrate my own stories, and conquer my Everest!

Skydive Dubai: Where the Dream Met Reality

The day had finally come! 17th January 2015.

A heady mix of adventure, fear, thudding heartbeats, and tension on the face described me. I asked myself one final time, "Are you sure you want to go ahead with this"? I convinced myself it was natural that I was going through this and allowed myself to ignore it all.

Iaona was sitting beside me and smiled when I looked up. I smiled back. At 6,000 feet, she checked my parachute and all the equipment. At 10,000 feet, I prepared myself, wore my goggles and helmet, and checked my altimetre. It was constantly moving clockwise to reach its pinnacle at 12,000'. Jumpers sitting closest to the gate opened the shutter. The first one popped out, and then the second and third. My heart leaped to my mouth. I kept a brave face and displayed no emotion. Despite the 7-second gap between each jumper, my chance came much too soon, and I knew something big was going to happen within the next minute.

Iaona helped me to the aircraft door, and I stood sideways, halfway outside the door, looking in the direction of the movement, as was taught to me, with both legs one behind the other, holding the door with one hand on top of the other.

Two instructors jump with the student during the first three jumps, holding and flying with him on either side. The second instructor, an ex-British paratroop sergeant, stood outside the gate holding my left hand. Iaona held my right hand and signalled me to start the 'Exit procedure'.

At 12,000 feet, when I stood half outside the door, I felt the wind slap me in the face. It was real now. There was no going back.

"Check out!" I shouted at the instructor, holding my left hand.

"Check in!" I yelled at Iaona on my right.

She smiled at me—one that said everything would be okay. At that moment, something inside me clicked. Fear evaporated, and I jumped.

For a second, I felt weightless, completely suspended in a space where the world ceased to exist. The desert stretched below me like an endless carpet, and I was part of the sky. But it was my first freefall, which happened too fast to grasp fully. Yet the exhilaration was undeniable. I landed smoothly and was met with congratulations.

The next one followed on the same day after a gap. The tension drained me, and I decided not to do more than two jumps daily. It went off well, and I was content with my first day.

Iaona was happy with my progress. I had made minor mistakes, but mostly, things were on the right track. My exit was generally fine, and I tried to look up at the aircraft, which was a good sign of exit. I was too rigid and making unnecessary movements in the air. The gushing air from below was too powerful. I was supposed to keep my body relaxed. However, I was destined to learn it the brutal way.

The Spin

It was my second day. I reached the Drop Zone very early in the morning. I wanted to have a cup of coffee at the canteen.

"It's $5." The canteen manager informed me.

"It's expensive, buddy," I calculated and left the canteen. Let me finish my third jump first.

Iaona met me at the Drop Zone. We practiced emergency drills and prepared ourselves for the jump. I was to fly in the fifth aircraft of the day, which would take another half an hour. I yearned for the coffee I had just missed at the canteen.

The third jump required no manoeuvres. This was the last mandatory jump with two instructors. Both instructors were supposed to leave me free and observe my solo fall. If I cleared this, I would graduate to jumping with a single instructor. But this would be the one that would test me in ways I hadn't imagined. It started like the others—check out, check in, and go. Everything seemed fine until, at 7,000 feet, I made an abrupt movement with my left hand while trying to watch my altimetre. The gushing air was unforgiving. It tilted my balance.

I started spinning uncontrollably, tumbling through the sky.

The moment my body twisted out of position, chaos ensued. My body started turning towards the left. Within a second, I was tumbling and taking barrel rolls, falling completely out of control. During the fall, I realized I was looking up at the sky instead of the usual belly-down position. My heart started pounding in my chest as the world spun violently around me.

Iaona had taught me during emergency drills in the morning. "Get your one hand in front of your stomach if you find yourself facing the sky instead of the earth."

I remembered and tried to bring one hand in front of my stomach to turn upside, but to no avail. I was simply tumbling and rolling. My legs got straightened in the process, and my fall grew faster.

I could see Iaona trying to stabilize me, but I spun away each time she got close. I remember kicking her twice in the process. She couldn't keep up with my speed. I was falling faster than she could reach, and I was on my own now. The ground was approaching too quickly, and with every spin, my mind raced through survival instincts.

To my surprise, I found that I was not afraid even in those moments so close to death. I knew I had seconds to act before everything could go terribly wrong.

It must be around 3,500 feet when I said to myself, "Enough is enough. Let me pull the parachute."

I knew that this manoeuvre was dangerous, as there was a possibility of the parachute wrapping your body and creating a fatal emergency. But I had lost all options. Someone had to save me.

I pulled the parachute.

And then, with a miracle, the parachute deployed, and I found myself floating in the air, the musical sound of a flapping parachute just over me. The ground was just a thousand feet below. I was saved by a mere 5 seconds!

Relief and Resolve

Not surprisingly, I reached the Drop Zone early and landed pretty well. We went to our debriefing room to find out what happened and why. I had learned a lot of lessons. The experience was traumatic. However, I had never found myself scared. Even in the air, my mind had been ticking even though I was out of control of the fall. This seemed like good news. I was proud of myself.

Iaona met me in the debriefing room. She looked at me; her relief mirrored my own.

"I am so happy to see you alive," she said.

"So am I," I responded.

"So, do we go for the jump again?"

I paused, took a breath, and smiled.

"Yes," I said. "But first, I need a coffee."

I wanted to have at least a cup of coffee before I died!

What an irony! I had refused a cup of coffee to myself in the morning, which cost me $5, whereas I had just failed the third jump, which cost me $450 and my life. I had to repeat my jump.

Some lessons are learned in exciting ways.

I was also convinced that there was an angel I called God, who looked after me through all the crises. I could feel His presence close to me. I was sure that my dying was not going to happen so soon.

That short break allowed me to reflect. This wasn't just about jumping anymore; it was about survival. It was about pushing through trauma and facing fear head-on.

Back to the Sky

Two hours later, I was back in the air. This time, I was prepared. The manager had gone through the emergency drills with me, and as I boarded the plane, I felt an eerie calm. The fear had dulled, replaced by determination.

The repeat of the third jump went off very well. Though I was still tight in the air, everything happened right. To ensure I didn't destabilize again, the manager stayed close and held me whenever I strayed. I was back on the ground, thoroughly impressed with myself. I knew one thing: I would always get back up no matter how hard the fall.

Going back up again on the same day of the trauma and getting it right was one of my most significant achievements on the way to conquering my Everest. I was holding onto the rock with my fingernails. But quitting was out of the question!!

Skydiving had pushed me to my limits, but it had also shown me that those limits could be stretched. It wasn't just about conquering my Everest—it was about conquering myself.

Years passed. Akshaj grew up to be a fine young boy. One day, he approached me and said, “Dad, I want to go skydiving.”

The world had taken a full circle.

I put up a brave front, as he was my weakness.

“Go ahead, buddy. You will find me with you whenever you want.”

As I write this, Akshaj has already obtained the B certificate from the US Parachute Association. I am so proud that he is so much better than me.